Editing
Secrets
of
Best-Selling
Authors

Kathy Ide

Lighthouse Publishing
of the Carolinas
ShopLPC.com

EDITING SECRETS OF BEST-SELLING AUTHORS BY KATHY IDE
published by LPCBooks
a division of Iron Stream Media
100 Missionary Ridge, Birmingham, AL 35242

ISBN: 978-1-64526-274-9
Copyright © 2020 by Kathy Ide
Cover design by Ted Ruybal
Interior design by AtriTex Technologies P Ltd

Available in print from your local bookstore, online, or from the publisher at ShopLPC.com.

For more information on this book and the author, visit KathyIde.com.

Brought to you by the creative team at LPCBooks.com:
Denise Loock, Shonda Savage, and Stephen Mathisen.

Library of Congress Cataloging-in-Publication Data
Ide, Kathy.
Editing Secrets of Best-Selling Authors / Kathy Ide 1st ed.

Printed in the United States of America.

PRAISE FOR
EDITING SECRETS OF
BEST-SELLING AUTHORS

I wish everyone who had submitted a manuscript to me as an acquisitions editor had read this book first. What helpful tips and techniques to boost your writing to the next level!

—Erin Taylor Young
Author, Podcaster, Speaker, Blogger
Co-host of Write from the Deep

The content in *Editing Secrets* is golden! These practical strategies will help authors improve their craft and polish their manuscripts. Simply put, Kathy Ide's ideas will make your writing better.

—Margot Starbuck
Developmental Editor and Ghostwriter
Author of *Writing Query Letters that Shine*

I'm always looking for a good source of writing/editing information to recommend to my editing clients. I hit the jackpot with *Editing Secrets of Best-Selling Authors*. If you're looking to strengthen your manuscript from sentence to story, this book has so much valuable information, I can't tell you how much I love it.

—Lori Freeland
Author/Editor/Writing Coach

As a professional editor and writer, I found this book full of helpful information.

—Linda Nathan
Owner, Logos Word Designs, LLC,
Writing, Editing, and Consultation Services

It is no secret that Kathy Ide has written *the* book for authors, bloggers, editors, journalists, marketers, and students. Readers will learn better word choices, effective sentence construction, and how to show a story rather than merely tell it. I am a much better writer for having read, resourced, and referenced this invaluable book. And it will help you unwrap your writing gifts too.

—Tom Siebert
Writer and Editor

Editing Secrets of Best-Selling Authors is an excellent resource, especially for aspiring authors hoping to turn professional. This book includes a comprehensive primer on the many layers and facets of the editorial process, sandwiched between gold nuggets of advice from authors who have traveled the road before us. If you're looking to take your writing—and your career—to the next level, this is the book for you.

—Lindsay A. Franklin
Best-selling Author of *The Story Peddler*
Award-Winning Freelance Editor

ACKNOWLEDGMENTS

In my twenty years as a professional freelance editor, I've worked with numerous writers on a vast array of projects. While I hope they all learned and gained some valuable tips from my edits, I learned a lot from them as well. I'm a much better editor today because of what my clients taught me along the way.

I am grateful to the authors and other publishing industry professionals I've met at writers' conferences over the years ... and especially thankful for the folks who worked hard to put on those conferences. Even more so now that I direct two of them and understand how much time and effort goes into planning and presenting them.

I'm particularly appreciative of the best-selling authors who graciously shared their editing tips with me and granted permission to quote them in this book.

Even with all the professional contacts I've made in this exciting industry, this book would not be possible without the faithful support of my wonderful husband, Richard, who finds ways to amuse himself while I'm working on my writing, editing, and conference directing ... and yet thoroughly enjoys my company whenever I'm available to spend time with him.

FOREWORD

There are many aspects to writing a book and many trails each writer has to take before his or her first book is published. A part of my personal writing journey was meeting Kathy Ide at my first writers' conference. Over the years following that initial meeting, she was a skilled mentor and a determined encourager for me.

During that time, I discovered that in one way, writing is similar to dieting and exercising. Planning and promising to do it is one thing, usually a necessary part of the process, but until we actually follow through, not stopping until we've figured out what works and what doesn't, there will be nothing but lip service to show for it. Like dieting and exercising, once we know what we're capable of and mix that with what works for our bodies, we have to faithfully devote time to the plan. That may sound like a bit of a turnoff. But if we writers hope to captivate an audience for five to fifteen hours of their valuable time, it will take a lot of hard work on our part.

I spent years working on my first novel, trying to learn how to get the story that was inside me onto the written page in a way that looked anything like what I saw inside my head and felt in my heart. Even when I knew a scene well in my mind, I couldn't get it onto paper with the same power it had when I imagined it. That takes practice ... and gleaning from many writing resources.

Editing Secrets of Best-Selling Authors is one of those resources. I hope you'll allow Kathy Ide to help you become the best writer possible, not just in the mechanics of editing but also in the important steps of how to process and apply the creative side of writing.

—Cindy Woodsmall

TABLE OF CONTENTS

INTRODUCTION

Congratulations! You've created the first draft of a book—or at least the first few chapters of one—and you're reasonably happy with what you've come up with. You wrote from your heart, pouring words, thoughts, and emotions onto paper—well, into a Word document, anyway—and you finally have a solid start on a complete manuscript.

Now it's time to look critically at what you've written to figure out how to make it even better. Editing involves viewing your "baby" objectively—as objectively as a mommy or daddy can—and determining how to make it stronger, healthier, and more powerful so it can reach its full potential.

Successful writers spend a lot more time editing than they do writing. They know that what they write from the heart needs to be analyzed by the mind to make it the best it can be. To ensure that the story or message they want to convey comes across clearly and effectively.

I've been writing for publication since 1989, and I've been a professional freelance editor since 1998. A lot of what I learned about writing and editing came from books, from workshops at writers' conferences, from personal experience, from my critique groups, and from best-selling authors I've had the privilege of coming to know during my years in the publishing industry. In this book, I'm going to share with you some of the editing secrets I discovered along the way.

Numerous writing and editing books have been published—and I suggest you read them too. Appendix A has a list of my personal recommendations. In this book you'll find tips from actual best-selling authors who have studied editing techniques and implemented them, resulting in books that have reached the hearts and touched the lives of many readers. *Editing Secrets of Best-Selling Authors* is a collection of tips they believe are the most important aspects of editing a manuscript.

In addition to direct quotes from best-selling authors, I've included my own suggestions based on comments I've heard repeatedly from multi-published authors, agents, and publishers.

Writing captivating stories—whether in fiction, memoir, or anecdotes—requires special techniques. Therefore, the section on editing fiction is divided into multiple chapters. Even if you're writing nonfiction, your manuscript will benefit tremendously if you learn and use fiction techniques in your anecdotes. Even if you plan to write nonfiction exclusively, don't skip the fiction tips. Wherever you see terms like *character* or *plot,* remember they can refer to real individuals and events or made-up people and situations.

Best-selling authors will admit there's no pat formula to "success." What works for one author doesn't always work for others. However, if you're an aspiring, beginning, or intermediate writer, the tips in this book will help you polish your manuscript and get it ready for publication—whether you hope to attract a traditional publisher or take the self-publishing route. If you're an established author, these tips can help you edit other writers' manuscripts, either in a critique group setting or as an editorial freelancer.

By applying these techniques, you can turn that rough draft into a masterpiece!

Best-selling author Julie-Allyson Ieron says:

Does *edit* evoke images of a mad doctor opening his satchel of leeches above your fresh page of healthy prose with the intent of bleeding out its life?

It isn't as bad as all that. A good edit eliminates distracting words, wasted space, rabbit trails, careless errors, and fluff that try a reader's patience because they're packed with what my Weight Watchers instructor would call empty calories.

I am a tougher editor on my own work than any publisher's editor has ever been. I don't settle for anything less than vibrant writing where every word carries its weight, where not one could I eliminate without doing damage to the reader's experience. Most of my best work I write a third to a half longer than my target word count. Then I force out every sentence, word, space, or comma that isn't crucial. Finally I find myself right at word count, with a tighter, clearer chapter or article.

Tight writing, sharp writing, fresh writing isn't about the writing at all. It's about getting the writing out of the way so, like the silver bullet of a passenger train, the message shimmers as it zips along a smooth track to the reader's heart.

Chapter 1

WHY EDIT?

Writing the first draft of a new book can be great fun. Inspiration sparks an idea, and you tap into your creative nature to develop the content or storyline. As you string words into sentences, build sentences into paragraphs, and form paragraphs into sections and chapters, you imagine opening readers' minds and finding a place in their hearts.

⊰∻⊱

Best-selling author Cindy Woodsmall says:

The concept of writing is so simple, really—connect sentences in such a way that they tell a story that entertains and changes the reader. Despite the simplicity of the action, writing takes focused effort. Writers must use the nontangible assets of mind, heart, and will to create a tangible product.

Whether stories bubble up inside us, begging to be written, or we are digging deep so we can cup our hands and come up with a bit of water, a good writer does what it takes to write the best possible story.

⊰∻⊱

No first draft is ever the best it can be. Therefore, no first draft is ready for publication. Regardless of what your publishing plans are.

If you submit your manuscript to a traditional publisher, your competition will be stiff. Publishing houses receive a constant stream of submissions, so they can afford to be extremely picky.

If a manuscript, query letter, or proposal isn't highly polished, an acquisitions editor will immediately reply with a form-letter rejection ... or simply send the submission to the recycle bin.

If your plan is subsidy publishing (paying a company to do the typesetting, interior design, and cover, then putting your book out there for people to buy), you want to make sure your words say what you intended them to say in the most powerful and effective way possible. You also want to avoid the embarrassment of putting out a substandard product. And please don't add to the proliferation of badly written (aka poorly edited) books taking up shelf space in used bookstores!

Even if you're only going to self-publish for family and friends, consider this: Your book will likely be passed down from generation to generation. You don't want it filled with mistakes that could've been avoided with some good self-editing.

Two Sides of the Brain

Scientific studies have shown that the human brain has two distinct sides, or hemispheres, each responsible for a different type of thinking. The right side of the brain specializes in intuitive, creative, subjective thoughts. The left side focuses on logical, rational, analytical, technical, and objective thinking.

Almost everyone uses both sides of his or her brain. But few people are equally adept at both. Most of us have a distinct bent for one style of thinking or the other.

Predominantly right-brained readers enjoy books that tug on their emotions, such as romance novels and character-driven stories, nonfiction books about life issues, or inspiring devotionals. Left-brained readers tend to prefer how-to books, Bible studies, or plot-driven fiction.

Right-brainers rarely notice typos or errors in punctuation, usage, grammar, and spelling when they're reading. And if they do notice, the mistakes don't bother them much. But for left-brainers, errors jump off the page. They're usually so distracted by errors, they have a hard time getting past them—or staying quiet about them.

Most people who do substantive content editing or overall critiques are right-brainers. Those who do copyediting or proofreading for a living are strong left-brainers.

Typically, right-brained authors are "seat of the pants" writers. They get a spark of an idea and start writing, with no clear direction in mind. They go with the flow and see what develops. Left-brained people are usually planners/plotters. They have to outline before they start writing so they know where the book is headed. They create chapter-by-chapter synopses, character sketches, and timelines.

This difference comes to light in many areas of life. Right-brained people enjoy spontaneity. For them, the perfect vacation would be to hop in the car and drive, and when they feel like stopping, stop. They assume they'll find lodging when they need it—and if they don't, no big deal. Traveling is an adventure, right?

But left-brained people need to plan vacations—where they're going, how they'll get there, where they'll stop along the way, what activities they'll do each day, and how and when they're coming home.

Successful writers have to use both sides of the brain ... or hire people to help them with the tasks that don't come as naturally. Even mainly right-brained people can benefit from outlining and creating character sketches, whether they do it before much writing is done or after they've completed a full first draft. And left-brainers realize that no matter how much planning they do ahead of time, stories often take on a life of their own and go in different directions than anticipated. These writers have to allow for changes along the way.

The Writing and Editing Dance

Whether you're predominantly right- or left-brained, you want to write the first draft of a manuscript from the heart. When you start writing something new, you need to access your right brain, the creative side, to come up with ideas to write about.

As you work on your first draft, let your heart flow freely on the page. Don't worry about whether it's good, or if everything's punctuated properly, or if all the words are spelled right. Don't concern yourself with sentence structure or best word choices. Don't do anything to stop the creative flow. Just let it come. Fly through that rough draft and get it all out.

If you're a predominantly left-brained person, lock up your internal editor as you write the first draft ... with a promise that you'll let him out after you've finished so he can revise and improve it.

Clear Communication

Did you know that more women buy books than men? Whether that's true or not, I wrote that question to make a point about clear communication. Grammatically, the sentence could mean there are more women who buy books than there are women who buy *men*. While that may also be true, it's not what you thought when you read that the first time, is it?

This is an example of why it's so important to edit your manuscript. You need to analyze what you've written to make sure it clearly and logically expresses what you meant to say.

Edit Everything

Edit everything you write that you want someone else to read. In addition to your book manuscript and any articles you want to submit for publication, you should also edit your blogs, newsletters, social media posts, and even emails.

Okay, if you're sending an email to a close friend who won't notice, won't care, or will laugh good-naturedly about your typos or misspelled words, you don't need to edit. Then again, you might want to ... if only to avoid any unintended meanings in your message.

The way you edit depends on the type of material you're editing. Emails and texts can be chatty, can include lots of exclamation points, can use words in all caps. But you still want to make sure that what you wrote comes across the way you intended.

Chapter 2

WHEN TO EDIT

Some people like to write the full manuscript before they do any editing. Others prefer to edit as they go. Strongly left-brained writers may have trouble moving on to chapter 2 until they feel comfortable that chapter 1 is the best it can be, at least for now.

Work in whatever way is best for you. There's no right or wrong method.

Your Body Clock

We all have different times of day when we're at our most creative and when we're best at being analytical. Consider your personal body clock. What are your optimal times for writing? What are your best times for editing? Now, what do you usually do during those times? Not sure? Keep a diary or take notes when you edit or write and see when you're most productive.

Of course, everyone has daily responsibilities. If you have a job, you're required to be at work on a particular schedule. If you have kids, they need you at specific times. But we also all have blocks of optional time in our calendars, and we choose what we want to do with those. How do you typically fill those slots? Do you need to make adjustments to fit in time to edit?

Analyze the time of day when you're most creative and when you're most analytical. Write when you feel most creative; edit when you feel most analytical.

Maximize Your Efforts

You can maximize your editing alertness by taking care of yourself physically. You know the usual advice: get plenty of rest, drink lots of water, take regular breaks, exercise. Maintaining good physical health is important in both the writing process and the editing process. (For more on this, see my book *Typing without Pain*.)

Besides helping you avoid repetitive strain injuries, taking breaks can keep your brain at its peak. Editing can be mentally exhausting—especially if you're a mostly right-brained person. Make sure to give yourself some time off.

If you've been accessing your creative side in the writing process, you'll also need a break to effectively switch to the analytical editing process.

Best-selling author Eva Marie Everson says:

After I write long sections (I crank out about three thousand words at a time), I step away for at least half a day. The next morning (or the next time I sit to work), I go back over what I wrote the day before. My mind now reads as a *reader*, not as the *writer*. I strengthen the section by removing unnecessary words, adding and removing action tags, replacing weak works with stronger ones, etc. I try to see the scene or scenes as if they are playing out in front of me, which helps a great deal.

Letting some time go by after you write allows your brain to be more objective than if you launch straight from writing mode into editing mode. If you try to edit right after you've written something, your brain will fill in the gaps—you'll read what you know you meant rather than what you actually put on the page.

Best-selling author James Scott Bell says:

Put some distance between you and your work-in-progress before the first read-through. For at least three weeks, forget about it. Work on other projects. When you come back to your WIP, read it through as if you were a reader with a new book. Take only minimal notes; don't do any revising. Your first job is to get an overall sense of the story as a story.

Best-selling author Kathleen Y'Barbo says:

Print out the manuscript and do a complete read-through in hard copy. Aloud. This is how you will know what's there. Take notes as you read, but don't stop to rewrite. Just read. Save the edits for later.

Editing with Others

The saying goes "It takes a village to raise a child." Your manuscript is no different. It takes a team to produce a high-quality book. And that team doesn't start when you're ready to get assistance with typesetting, cover design, printing, and marketing. It begins as soon as you've done some writing—at the very latest, when you've completed the first draft of your manuscript.

If no one but you has seen what you've written, show it to some people you trust to be totally honest with you. What's clear in your mind may be confusing in someone else's. Often a fresh pair of eyes can see mistakes you can't, simply because you're too close to the work.

It's okay to seek advice from close friends and family members. But loved ones are often hesitant to say anything negative about your work, even if they detect that something is off, for fear of hurting your feelings. They will probably tell you that your writing is brilliant, inspired, fantastic. That's great. Every writer needs a reliable base of enthusiastic encouragers. But those people probably won't be able to help you understand how to improve your manuscript.

Show what you've written to some representatives of your target audience—the people who might buy your book even though they don't know you. If you're writing a novel for teen girls, for example, have a few teenage girls read it. They'll feel honored that you asked for their opinions, and they'll let you know whether what you wrote rings true for them. If your book is for mothers of preschoolers, show your manuscript to some moms of toddlers. Ask for their honest feedback. What parts did they find helpful? Which sections were confusing, distracting, or boring? What else do they think you should include?

Consider these assessments as objectively as you can. If you disagree with one person's opinion, ask someone else. If you receive the same feedback from more than one reviewer, give it serious consideration.

But don't stop there. Your target readers may be fantastic when it comes to helping you shape your content. But if they're not writers, they may not understand *why* certain sections are confusing or distracting ... and they probably won't know how to fix those problems.

For more objective feedback on your work, show your manuscript to one or more fellow authors. If you're not part of a critique group, find some writers who live near you—preferably ones who are in about the same stage of their writing journey you are—and meet with them on a regular basis. Weekly, monthly, whatever best fits your schedules. If you don't know any writers in your geographic vicinity, connect with some online and communicate via email.

In a critique group, members share their manuscripts with one another and offer suggestions for improvement. Each person will have a different perspective. And they'll all contribute something unique based on the writing books, websites, workshops, conferences, and classes they've learned from.

Giving and receiving feedback with like-minded people can sharpen your writing and self-editing skills. And it won't cost you anything but time.

～≈≈※≈≈～

Best-selling author Eva Marie Everson says:

I have good "crit partners"—the select few I trust to read my work and give honest feedback. They know my voice and are firm yet gentle in the critiques they offer. A writer who refuses critique is missing a golden opportunity. No one, shy of God, writes it perfectly the first time. No one.

～≈≈※≈≈～

After you've incorporated any suggested changes as you see fit, read your piece aloud multiple times. How do the changes sound to you? Remember, this is your book. You have the final word. Carefully consider all feedback offered, but in each instance, give yourself the freedom to take it or leave it.

Editing with a Professional

Finally, I suggest hiring a professional freelance editor to review your manuscript and proposal before submitting them to a publisher. That can greatly improve your chances of acceptance. Even if you already have a contract with a publishing house, you don't want to appear as anything less than a professional at your craft. In addition, if the editor hired by the publishing house to work on your manuscript has to spend too much time finding errors you should have caught yourself, you could miss your typesetting deadline, which might push back your publication date considerably. (More on this in chapter 19.)

Prepare Yourself

Before you start editing, get both sides of your head ready for the process by nurturing what comes naturally for you and developing what doesn't.

For Right-Brained Writers

If you're mostly right-brained by nature, you can enhance the left side of your brain by doing crossword puzzles, other word challenges, or games like Boggle, Scrabble, Hangman, Wheel of Fortune, and Words with Friends. Number games, like Solitaire, don't deal with words or even letters, but they encourage your brain to use logic and organizational skills.

Playing word games with strongly left-brained people can be irritating ... and frustrating when they win most of the time. Either overcome that obstacle for the sake of your craft or find other right-brainers who will play with you.

For Left-Brained Writers

If you're predominantly left-brained, the most difficult part of the editing process might be to take the technically accurate material you've written and breathe life into it. If you're not careful, you can edit your wonderful first draft to death.

As you prepare to edit, and from time to time during the editing process, do something to stir your creativity and refresh your inspiration—especially when you've reached that third, fourth, or twentieth revision.

To access the creative side of your brain, engage in exercises that spark your imagination. Play charades. Draw and color a picture that illustrates a plot idea or point in your book. Even if you're writing nonfiction, find story-starter questions (aka writing prompts) and contemplate the ones you find intriguing.

New York Times best-selling novelist Cindy Woodsmall has a few methods that help stir creativity and refresh her when she's weary. One way in which she finds inspiration, for both writing and editing, is by reading poetry.

In *Poems of Quotes*, Gary R. Hess states that there are fifty-five types of poetry.[1] Other sources indicate there are close to double that number. With a little effort, you should be able to find at least one type that nourishes your soul.

Another activity Cindy finds helpful to tap into the creative side of the brain is to put Moving Art on a television screen where she can see it whenever she glances up from her computer. This has medical advantages as well. Doctors say that looking away from the computer screen a few times per hour helps with dryness and headaches.

Cindy says:

> Whenever I glance up, I see footage of oceans, deserts, mountains, waterfalls, forests, sunrises/sunsets, etc. Some of these videos cost money. Others are free through YouTube or Amazon Prime. It's incredibly refreshing anytime but can save your sanity when you're working fourteen-hour days to meet a deadline!

Nature videos have their own music. For those that don't, Cindy likes to put on instrumental music. "Some writers listen to music with words," she says, "but that messes with my head and makes it harder to write ... unless I'm using it to help me tune out the world around me, which has its time and place too."

[1] http://www.poemofquotes.com/articles/poetry_forms.php.

Best-selling author Suzanne Woods Fisher says:

Identify your habits in your work. Every writer has them: tendencies to spit out sentences in a certain way, favorite go-to words, a signature punctuation. Identify your habits ... and then edit them out. Don't confuse a unique voice with writing habits.

Chapter 3

CONTENT EDIT

In this editing level, you're going to analyze the material you've decided to put into your manuscript to see if it contains everything you need ... and nothing you don't.

The Outline

If you're a planner/plotter, you probably started with an outline of your manuscript—a "map" to organize your thoughts—before you wrote the first word.

If you're a "seat of the pants" writer, you probably began with a passion burning in your heart, a blinking cursor on a blank screen, and a general concept of who, what, where, when, how, and why. You started typing—or maybe writing in a spiral notebook if you're old-school—with no more than a vague idea of what you were going to end up with.

If you haven't already created an outline, make one now. If you did, go through it and see if it matches what you wrote. For each chapter, write a summary paragraph of the main point (for nonfiction) or everything that happens (for fiction or memoir).

Now, study the outline.

For Nonfiction

Ask yourself if every chapter, as well as everything in each chapter, fits the main message you want to convey in this book.

Analyze every portion of your book, asking yourself, *Does this really need to be there?* Does it fit with the theme, purpose, and topic? Does it present new information, or is it restating something you've presented in a different section? If you've addressed the same issue elsewhere in the book, either combine the two sections or remove one of them.

For Fiction

Do you have a chapter in which nothing much happens? Could it be deleted without affecting the storyline? If you need to convey some information contained in that chapter, consider weaving in those details through relevant, interesting action in a different chapter.

Best-selling author Julie-Allyson Ieron says:

You need to focus on the key point of your book. A plethora of sidetracks will tempt you to scatter your thoughts and disorganize your logic. But you need to stay the course if you want readers to "get it."

After writing the first two chapters of a novel recently, I sent them along to my first reader—expecting accolades and congratulations all around.

I had tried to be artistic, hopscotching deftly across years and continents. But my reader couldn't make the leaps of logic required to understand the story. I needed to lead her along plausibly, smoothly. When I made that adjustment in the next draft, I hooked her on my story and made her care about my characters.

Whether you're writing fiction or nonfiction, take the one theme that unites your piece, organize supporting points in a logical flow, and transition smoothly to bring readers along with you. Every observation, story, quote, and instruction needs to move the overall purpose along.

Research

For Nonfiction

In addition to sharing your own thoughts, ideas, and stories, support your points with input from other sources.

Read through your manuscript, looking for places where objective backup would be beneficial. Then talk to people who may be able to provide it. Search the internet for legitimate, trustworthy, objective information, details, corroborating facts, and statistics.

As you research, you'll find all sorts of interesting tidbits of information. Resist the temptation to include everything you discover. Weave in only what's relevant, pertinent, and essential to your point.

If you're overwhelmed with the desire to share extraneous facts, consider moving them to a separate section at the end of your book. Or put them on your website. Lists and quizzes created from these extra details could make great content for your newsletter ... or be used to attract readers to sign up for your newsletter. If you have a lot of additional material, there may be enough to start a whole new book.

For Fiction

If you think only nonfiction authors need to research, think again. Nothing discredits a novelist faster than incorrect details.

Research all locations and settings mentioned in your story to make sure they're described authentically. If the story is set in a fictional town that's part of a real state or country, make sure the weather, the flora and fauna, and other details are accurate.

Also research your main characters' careers. How do people in those professions talk, act, and think? How do they handle the tools they use in that line of work? Do the same with hobbies, pastimes, family dynamics, etc.

For example, considering your character's geographical background and upbringing, would he refer to the midday meal as lunch, dinner, or supper? What would he call the evening meal? Ask a family member, friend, or colleague who lives in that area or look for the answer online (somewhere more reliable than Wikipedia).

Here's another example. How do you refer to your favorite carbonated beverage? Do you call it soda? Pop? Soda pop? Soft drink? Do you call it a Coke even if it's not Coca-Cola? This may seem like unimportant minutia, but readers who are familiar with the settings in your novel will notice.

If your characters don't all hail from places you've lived, figure out what they'd call their drinks. How do you find that out? Believe it or not, there's a website that shows what terms people in different parts of the country use for their soft drinks. Check out "Soda vs. Pop vs. Coke: Who Says What, and Where?"[2]

Oh, and if you use Coca-Cola in your manuscript, make sure you've spelled it the way The Coca-Cola Company does. Do the same with any other brand names or trademarks. Companies are quite particular about correct representation of their products.

Company owners also get upset when their products are presented in a negative light. If you have a character who despises Olive Garden, have another character love it. If a character's Volvo is a clunker, she could be discouraged that it's not as reliable as the Volvo she used to own.

As with nonfiction, include only those details that are directly relevant to your story.

Best-selling author Gail Gaymer Martin says:

Sometimes authors read something interesting about a person, location, or situation and want to use it in their novels because they think readers will be as intrigued as they are. Mark a skull and crossbones over any research or general information that does not directly relate to the focus of your story. Every scene and sentence must have a purpose in moving the story forward.

---

[2] https://www.huffpost.com/entry/soda-vs-pop_n_2103764.

Giving the history of an old building, over-describing the attire of a secondary character, or providing details of a historic battle scene can be detrimental to the story's pace. If the reader stops to ponder an irrelevant piece of information—wondering why the author described the old building or secondary character in detail or why the waiter wore an apron—the author has jerked the reader from the story.

Keep your research and information crucial. If there are things you want to share with the reader, add a For Your Information section at the end of your novel and provide the details there for the history buffs.

Symbolism

Look through your manuscript for opportunities to incorporate symbolism. Can a *thing* mentioned in the story represent what's happening in the story or within the main character?

For example, you may show a character picking a beautiful red apple off a tree in the first chapter. Life is great. But the character encounters a series of difficulties, and the next time he sees the tree, it's been ravaged by frost, which has made all the apples brown and wrinkled. Life isn't so good anymore. The woman he loves has left him, and his existence seems meaningless. This could be illustrated by the tree losing its leaves, its branches now bare and black. With the return of the character's ladylove, the tree could sprout a bit of green again. As they nurture this relationship, he nurtures the apple tree back to life. He breathes deeply of the scent of apple blossoms, and the future is full of promise again. In the final chapter, he and his girlfriend could be sitting under the tree, enjoying juicy red apples—and each other.

Similes and Metaphors

Look for places in your manuscript where you can replace flat writing with something more interesting, perhaps even poetic if that fits your character's personality.

For example, if you wrote, "The song was pretty," you could change it to "The hymn was a breath of fresh air to her spirit" (metaphor) or "The powerful chorus echoed in her mind like waves crashing onto the shore of her soul" (simile).

Don't overdo this technique. Use it sparingly for maximum effect—an occasional sprinkle here and there to spice up your writing.

Humor

If you can make readers laugh, you'll have an easier time making them cry ... or experience other emotions.

Best-selling author Gail Gaymer Martin says:

"Laughter is the best medicine," an old saying goes, and it holds truth. Chuckles and laughs promote physical health by using body muscles often neglected in regular exercise.

Shakespeare always added humorous scenes to his tragedies. It's called comic relief. Humor can happen with wordplay, pratfalls, and exaggeration.

Think of situations and events in your life that made you laugh at the time or after some time passed. Re-create a similar situation in your book to bring these moments to life.

Laughter is also a release from stress, grief, shame, and loneliness. Difficult situations that pull at the heartstrings help readers release their own pent-up emotions and often help them realize they aren't the only ones who feel alone, embarrassed, or duped. Humor in the face of such dire situations shows readers how they can resolve their issues and come out triumphant.

Ever notice how many serious movies, especially ones with deep or dark tones, have a comic-relief character who brings a touch of humor and lightness to the story? Humor is a shortcut to a viewer's or reader's emotions, and if you tap into their funny bone, you'll have easier access to their heartstrings as well.

Writing humor is a skill that requires attention and time to master. Study humor-writing techniques. And when you've written something you think is funny, show it to someone else to see if he or she agrees.

Best-selling author Renae Brumbaugh Green says:

When writing humor, timing is essential. Delay the punch line until the last possible moment. Writers can force a pause by inserting a new paragraph, even if the punch line is only a few words.

Whether fiction or nonfiction, go through your manuscript and look for places where a touch of humor or an amusing sidekick character might enhance your reader's experience.

Chapter 4

ORGANIZATIONAL EDIT

In this editing level, you're going to analyze how you've organized your manuscript to ensure the material is presented in a way that will have maximum impact on your readers.

Chapter Organization

Review your outline and consider the order in which chapters are presented. If a different order seems to make more sense, shift things around.

For Nonfiction

Even if your manuscript contains good information, the material must be presented logically so it flows well from one point to the next.

You may organize your material into lists, such as "Five Ways to ..." or "Ten Steps toward ...." If your material isn't how-to, consider whether it might be organized chronologically (in order of occurrence) or by some other natural sequence.

Break each main topic into three to five subtopics. Put all of your information under those headings and subheadings to divide the text into manageable chunks. Headings help readers transition from one subject to another.

Once you've established your categories, make sure everything under each subheading applies to that subject. Look at each paragraph or idea and determine where it belongs—or whether it belongs at all. This may require some reorganizing, but the results will be well worth the effort.

If you put everything you want to say on a topic together, wherever it fits best, you will avoid repetition.

For Fiction

The first chapter of a novel needs to hook the reader, riveting him or her to the page and creating an intense desire to read on and learn more about the characters and what happens to them. (See more in chapter 11.)

Chapter Beginnings

The way you start a chapter will determine whether someone reads the rest of what you wrote in that chapter.

For nonfiction, open each chapter by giving a clear overview of its content or an anecdote that illustrates the point of the chapter. Many nonfiction readers skip around, reading only the parts of a book that appear to best suit their immediate needs. Be sure your chapter titles are descriptive and appropriate. Intriguing opening paragraphs will entice people to read on.

For fiction, the first person mentioned at the beginning of every chapter must be the point-of-view character for that scene. (See chapter 13.) Give the reader enough description to visualize what the POV character sees without going into so much detail that the story gets bogged down. (See chapter 16.) And there has to be action—something happening—that engages the reader.

Chapter Middles

For nonfiction: After you've established your main point for the chapter, develop the point through sub-points that lead the reader from one step to the next.

For fiction: After you arouse reader curiosity by presenting an intriguing opening scene, add more details in subsequent paragraphs. Keep the action, conflict, and tension going. Something should be *happening* all the time. Weave in pertinent information in bits and pieces related to the action at the time. Avoid big chunks of backstory or description that aren't directly connected to what's going on in the scene.

Chapter Endings

For nonfiction, end each chapter with a brief summary of the material presented in the chapter—without repeating what you've already written. If you opened the chapter with an anecdote that illustrates the problem being addressed, you could close the chapter with a continuation of that anecdote, showing how the story ends.

For fiction, end every chapter with a cliffhanger, something that makes the reader turn the page because she can't wait to find out what happens next—no matter how late it is, how tired she is, or how much other stuff she has to do. Lure your readers into finishing one more chapter before they put the book down.

Best-selling author James Scott Bell says:

Look at the last few lines of each chapter. Often you can cut these and leave the reader with a page-turning feeling.

Scene Organization

For nonfiction, anecdotal scenes need to provide enough detail for readers to feel like the proverbial fly on the wall as they observe a snippet from your life or someone else's. This usually includes a brief description of where and when the scene took place, who was there, and what was observed (seen, heard, felt) by the person who experienced the story. Telling these stories in chronological order is better than flipping back and forth in time.

For fiction, every scene beginning should include a brief description of when and where the action takes place, who is there, and any other significant details, from the perspective of the point-of-view character.

Each scene should have a natural, logical ending. Don't end abruptly in the middle of a conversation or event, making readers feel like they missed something.

Best-selling author Deborah Raney says:

Spot-check first and last paragraphs. The first paragraph of each chapter should set the stage and paint a vivid image for the reader, as well as establish the scene's point-of-view character. The last paragraph of each chapter should contain some sort of hook, enticing the reader—and your editor—to keep turning pages. Quite often I discover that by deleting the last sentence of a chapter, I'm able to create a hook where none existed before. (If the deleted sentence contains crucial information, it may be incorporated in the next chapter.)

Sentence Organization

The actions in a sentence should be presented in the order in which they occur. Best-selling author Frank Ball offers this example:

"Is this seat taken?" Jack pointed at the chair.
(Jack wouldn't ask that question before pointing at the chair.)

Frank adds that phrases establishing time and place should precede the action so readers know where the characters are before they see characters doing things there. His example:

He reached to the highest shelf after stepping on the stool.

(Better: After stepping on the stool, he reached to the highest shelf.)

Sentence Beginnings

Watch for sentences that start with the same word(s), especially if they're close together. For example, instead of "Terry watched the sunset. Terry thought it was beautiful," you could write, "Terry watched the beautiful sunset."

Best-selling author Cecil Murphey says:

Too often when people read first-person accounts, they complain, "I got so tired of the *I, I, I* sentences."

Most people learned to read following the principle of the declarative sentence as subject, verb, and direct or indirect object. They tend to write the same way.

Someone once showed me a self-published memoir with twenty-eight sentences in a row that followed this pattern. (Twenty of them began with *I*.) Sentence twenty-nine began, "After that, I …," followed by seven more subject/verb sentences.

Analyze the sentences within each paragraph and find ways to vary their structure.

Sentence Endings

In addition to looking at how your sentences begin, consider how they end.

Best-selling author Gail Gaymer Martin says:

Speakers know that the last words they say are the ones remembered. In the same way, authors can read their narrative and dialogue with a discerning eye and structure sentences so that the prominent word ends the sentence. That way, the important word receives the power.

Sentence Length

Long, flowing sentences give readers a sense of meandering or pondering. Short, choppy sentences provide punch and urgency. Consider the tone you want to convey in each section of your book, and use short or long sentences to create the appropriate mood.

Best-selling author Gail Gaymer Martin says:

Sentences that are too long and complex can lose readers. If they have to stop and reread a sentence, you have pulled them from your novel and broken the spell of your story. Keep sentence length fluid. Long sentences work best during moments of introspection or in romantic descriptions. Short sentences work well for drama, suspense, and adventure.

Balance

Too much or too little of anything on a page can affect the flow.

For fiction, consider using different-colored highlights (on the screen or with a marker on printed pages) to identify backstory, setting, descriptions, dialogue, unspoken thoughts, observations, and actions.

For nonfiction, use different colors for your personal stories, other people's anecdotes, illustrations, statistics, objective observations, and driving home your points. This will give you an overall feel for which sections need to be shortened and which should be fleshed out.

Look at each page visually to make sure there's a balanced amount of white space versus text. Too little white space and your reader may feel overwhelmed. Too much can tempt a reader to skip or skim.

Best-selling author Gail Gaymer Martin says:

When you find flaws in the arrangement of your material, such as paragraphs that aren't cohesive and information presented in an illogical order, cut the dialogue or narrative into individual strips. Then move one into a different place and see if that's an improvement. Or cut the problem paragraphs and paste them into a new page, then organize them into a list of sentences. This gives you the ability to reorganize your dialogue or narrative and present the information in a more realistic, useful manner. By doing this, you may find ways to combine sentences, cut redundant phrases or lines, and place the information in a logical order.

Read It Aloud

At the end of your organizational edit, read your manuscript out loud. Or have someone read it to you. If you don't have a friend who can do this for you, find out if your computer or tablet has a text-to-speech option and use it.

Best-selling author Gayle Roper says:

Read your work out loud. Note awkward places for later rewriting. Also note places where you read something different from what's written. Often a rewrite comes to mind that's better than the original.

Chapter 5

COPYEDIT

In the copyedit stage, you'll use a literary "magnifying glass" to analyze every detail in your manuscript. In this process, your writing will become more tight, powerful, and effective.

Here are some specifics to look for.

Active vs. Passive

With *active voice*, the subject of a sentence performs an action. For example, "Theresa wrote a book." With *passive voice,* the subject of a sentence receives the action: "A book was written by Theresa."

An active sentence describes an action. For example, "Stuart threw a ball." A passive sentence indicates that something exists in a particular place: "A ball was in Stuart's hand."

Passive sentences typically include more words and may lead to a tangle of prepositional phrases. Passive voice can be vague and lifeless. Active voice and active sentences are typically clearer and keep readers more engaged.

To ferret out sentences where the subject is receiving an action, do a search for *by* phrases. If you find one that's in the passive voice, move the subject closer to the beginning of the sentence.

To find sentences that simply tell readers something exists, do a search for *is, was, are, were, be, been, would, could, has, had,* and *have.* Whenever you find one, consider replacing the passive sentence with one that describes an action that happens *to* someone or something.

Best-selling author Susan Meissner says:

Perform a word search for *was*. Remove as many you can, especially those that relegate your writing to the passive voice. For example, "The pavement was speckled by rain" is passive. "Rain speckled the pavement" says the same thing but is active and more engaging.

Here are some examples of how you can change weak, vague passive sentences into active ones.

Passive: Two cups of coffee *were* on the table.
Active: Joe *picked up* two cups of coffee from the table.

Passive: Andrew *had* dark, curly hair and a bushy beard.
Active: Andrew *ran* his fingers through his dark, curly hair, then *stroked* his bushy beard.

Best-selling author Gail Gaymer Martin says:

One of the main problems with passive sentences is that they tell rather than show. "She was beautiful." Can you picture that? Not really. But if you read, "Her long, raven-colored hair hung down her back in thick waves, contrasting with her eyes, the color of a Caribbean sea," you get a picture of this woman.

Instead of writing, "She was a ballerina," describe her entrance into the room. "She glided across the floor, her slender arms moving as fluidly as music, as if she'd worn her tutu for the evening."

Instead of "He was a cowboy," you could write, "His Stetson sat cocked on his head like a rooster's comb, reminding everyone he not only managed the ranch, he owned it." Much more vivid.

Sometimes passive voice is acceptable—even preferred. For example:

1. To emphasize the action rather than the subject

   Jim's marketing proposal *was approved* by the publicist.

2. To keep the subject and focus consistent throughout a passage

   The acquisitions editor presented a controversial story to the publishing committee. After long debate, the manuscript *was endorsed by* ...

3. To be tactful by not naming the subject

   The email *was misinterpreted.*

4. To describe a condition in which the subject is unknown or irrelevant to the sentence

   Every year, many people *are diagnosed* with diverticulitis.

5. To create an authoritative tone

   Visitors *are not allowed* after 9:00 p.m.

Clichés

A cliché is a word, phrase, or expression that has been used so much it has become overly familiar or commonplace.

The first time an author described a lawn as "manicured," that put a vivid descriptive image in the mind of the reader. But now the metaphor has been used so often it has become cliché. Same with "a single tear" rolling down a cheek. Using a different verb isn't enough to make this fresh.

Look for clichés in your manuscript. If you find one, come up with something original, something unique to you ... and to the POV character who's using it.

The only place clichés are acceptable is in the dialogue or internal monologue of a character who loves using them. Otherwise, you should avoid clichés like the plague. (Intentional cliché alert!)

Overused Actions

Look for actions you've used over and over in the manuscript. Here are a few common examples:

drinking coffee or tea

crying/weeping/sobbing

eyes widening

eyebrows lifting

forehead furrowing/creasing

frowning

smiling

nodding

shaking head

running fingers through hair

shrugging

sighing

If you (in nonfiction) or your characters (in fiction) are always doing the same things in the same locations, come up with more intriguing actions in a variety of interesting places. If you or your characters spend a lot of time crying, don't just use synonyms like weeping, sobbing, or shedding tears. Create a scene and situation, then show the character's thoughts about it in such a way that your reader *feels* the sadness. You won't have to tell readers about the crying. They'll know. And they'll feel like crying too.

Pet Words

Skim the pages of your manuscript and look for words that jump out because you've used them multiple times. When a word comes to your attention, do a search to see how often it appears. The more obscure the word, the fewer times it should be used in a manuscript. For example, words like *the* and *a/an* are "invisible"—readers gloss right over them. But words such as *obscure* should be used sparingly because they stand out.

Keep a list of the words and phrases you tend to overuse. Add to the list as you find new ones.

Best-selling author Gail Gaymer Martin says:

Authors tend to have favorite words. Run a Find and Replace on any word you overuse and select a synonym that works as well or better in each instance.

Pet phrases can also be a problem. Romance writers tend to use phrases such as *Her heart fluttered* or *Her pulse hammered*. Find new and more interesting ways to express those feelings.

Avoid repetitive nouns. For example, "John invited her in and motioned toward a chair. She crossed the room and sank into the chair." Instead of repeating *chair*, use *cushion* or *seat*.

This can also happen with verbs. In a long novel, you may find similar words and phrases used over and over: *He looked at her. He gazed at her. He eyed her. He studied her. He searched her face.*

Use a thesaurus to find alternatives to overused words. Better yet, rewrite sentences to convey what you meant to say in a clearer, more precise way.

Best-selling author Susan Meissner says:

Know your pet words and perform a Find and Replace at editing time. If you don't know your pet words, have someone read your manuscript looking only for them.

Weasel Words

A *weasel word,* according to Webster's online dictionary, is "a word used in order to evade or retreat from a direct or forthright statement or position."[3] But this phrase can also be used for any empty or useless word that weasels its way into your manuscript over and over.

Best-selling author Angela Hunt says:

The best tool for tracking down your weasel words is your word-processing program's Search and Replace feature. If you write in any of the standard programs—Word, Word Perfect, Scrivener, Pages—you will find Search (or Find) and Replace. When you're checking for a particular weasel word, ask your program to search for the word with spaces before and after it ... unless it's a word likely to be used several times at the end of a sentence—in that case, you'll want to omit the last space. Then ask it to replace that word with the same word in all capital letters—also with spaces before and after.

For instance, if I was searching for *that,* I would enter [space] that[space] in the Search box. Then I'd enter [space]THAT[space] in the Replace box.

---

[3] https://www.merriam-webster.com/dictionary/weasel%20word.

I do that for every weasel word on my list. This doesn't change any of my prose, but those weasel words now *loom* on the page and catch my attention as I work through subsequent drafts. And every time I see one, I stop and ask myself if I can make the sentence better by deleting or changing that word. If I can, great. If I can't—or if it would make the sentence too convoluted—the sentence remains as it was.[4]

The Worst Weasel Word

Angela goes on to identify what she considers to be the most common yet overlooked "weasel word."

Best-selling author Angela Hunt says:

The worst weasel word is one I first noticed the year I taught high school English. I'd never thought of it as a weasel word, but suddenly there it was, all over my students' papers. Can you guess what it was?

It!

It is so common we really don't think about it, but sometimes we fall into patterns that result in what I call "vague its." This particular species of *it* has infested many a sentence. When you find one of these, ask yourself, *What am I really trying to say here?*

Example: Mary wore a blue dress with flowers on *it*.

Does that *it* cause you to stop or slow down in any way? Probably not. Because you can tell immediately what *it* represents: the blue dress. So that's a good *it*. You could keep it. Although you'd earn some extra points by writing, "Mary wore a blue-flowered dress."

The *it* that weakens your prose is found in sentences like this:

---

[4] Angela Hunt, *Track Down the Weasel Words*, book 4 in the Writing Lessons from the Front series (Florida: Hunthaven Press, 2013).

It is hard to get a driver's license.

Hmm. What does that *it* stand for? You have to think a moment, don't you? *It* has no apparent connection to anything else in the sentence, the paragraph, or the world.

So back up and write what you're really trying to say: "Getting a driver's license is hard." Or complicated. Or whatever you really mean.

What about this example:

"You don't understand," Mom said, sniffling. "*It's* so hard to live without your dad."

In this example, the questionable *it* is in dialogue, and we loosen up when considering dialogue because people talk in all kinds of ways. If your character doesn't use proper grammar when she's crying and upset, that's typical of the human race. So let her keep her undefined *it*.[5]

❦

It is/was is a weak sentence beginning because the phrase contains a pronoun without a clear antecedent and a passive "telling" verb. For example, instead of writing "It was Princess Amber who said ...," write "Princess Amber said ..."

There is/are is similarly problematic. Instead of "There are four procedures that must be followed," write "Four procedures must be followed." Instead of "There was a long line of old shops on Main Street," write "Old shops lined Main Street."

Read All the Way Through

Read your manuscript from beginning to end to catch any mistakes that slipped in during this editing level. Look for places where you can improve the manuscript with more polishing.

---

[5] Ibid.

Best-selling author Lena Nelson Dooley says:

After I completely finish editing my manuscript, I read it out loud and mark places where I could add even more layers.

Chapter 6

SCISSORS EDIT

Any writing can be improved with a bit of tightening. Today's busy readers have short attention spans, so they're more likely to read books with small chapters divided into smaller subsections. Even long books can be popular if the writing is so tight that readers zip through the pages.

Excess words and phrases can bog down your writing, cloud your meanings, and diminish excitement. The tighter the writing, the more publishers—and readers—will like it.

In what I call a "scissors edit," you'll cut out everything that doesn't absolutely need to be in the manuscript. Analyze every word, phrase, sentence, and paragraph to see if any of them can be eliminated without changing the meaning. Use your editorial scissors to cut out anything that won't be missed. Your writing will be healthier without the excess "flab."

You may think there's nothing you could possibly delete from your beloved masterpiece. But consider the following suggestions. (Don't worry. Most of them won't be *too* painful.)

Boring Bits

For nonfiction, look for personal anecdotes that may be interesting to you and your family members but wouldn't necessarily hold the interest of someone who doesn't know you (unless family members are the only ones who will ever read the book). If a story doesn't apply to the majority of members in your target audience, take it out. Especially avoid anecdotes that are personal diatribes against people or situations.

For fiction, cut out anything that detracts from the action. Eliminate backstory that isn't essential to the scene it's in. If readers don't need to know the information till later, move it.

Consider whether any of your characters could be eliminated without adversely affecting the story. Perhaps two characters can be combined into one.

Take out small talk and unnecessary dialogue such as "Hello," "How are you?" "I'm fine, how are you?" "Good, thanks. How's the wife?" Meaningless chitchat destroys the momentum of the story. Skip to the part of the scene where something interesting is happening.

Where greetings are necessary, instead of nondescript ones like "Hi," have a character say something that increases the tension, such as "Thank God, you're home. We have to talk."

Stating the Obvious

For nonfiction, don't tell your readers things they already know, don't need to know, or can infer on their own.

Watch for phrases like "As we all know ..." If something would be obvious to the general public or common knowledge among people in your target audience, you don't have to point it out.

If you do feel the need to write something obvious, don't tell your readers you consider it superfluous. For example, instead of "As everyone knows, writing tight takes a lot of work," say, "Writing tight takes a lot of work."

Look for sentences that begin with phrases like "As you can see" or "Obviously" or "It should be clear to the reader" or "It goes without saying." If it goes without saying, don't say it.

For fiction, check your manuscript for author exposition—places where you've included something in dialogue or internal monologue only because you felt readers needed to know it.

Don't have a character tell others something they already know. For example: "As you recall, Father died last year."

Don't have characters talk about topics they wouldn't normally discuss. For example: "As long as no one digs up the box I buried, the secrets I wrote in my diary will remain private."

Don't include details a character wouldn't point out. For example: "After my boyfriend Michael Lapinski and I made out for twenty-five minutes in the backyard under the oak tree yesterday after school, he gave me a sixteen-inch-long gold chain with a tiny red heart on it."

Don't have a character say things that would be obvious to others. If someone barges into a room after being beaten with a baseball bat, don't have him say, "Look! I'm bleeding from my forehead." Instead, have him stumble in and ask for a bandage, or have another character react to the sight of him.

Weak Sentence Beginnings

Eliminate introductory phrases like "As a matter of fact," "As far as I'm concerned," "For the most part," "It is interesting to note that." If what you're about to say *isn't* interesting and factual, it shouldn't be there.

Unnecessary Words

If taking out a word or phrase does nothing to change the meaning of the sentence, delete it. Here are a few examples:

She nodded *her head.* (What else would she nod?)

He shook his head *no.* (Nodding is for yes; shaking of the head means no.)

I thought *to myself.* (You can't think *to* anyone else.)

He shrugged *his shoulders.*

Personally, I think … (All of your thoughts are personal.)

whether *or not*

each and every

He paced *back and forth*. (You can't pace *up and down*.)

twelve o'clock noon (or midnight)

exactly the same

She got out of *her* bed. (Unless she got out of someone else's bed.)

He looked *at his image* in the mirror. (Unless he's a vampire, that's what he'll see.)

Some "unnecessary" words may be helpful for cadence, style, or to show a character's personality. But if you don't have a specific reason for leaving them in, get out those scissors and snip away!

Throwaway Words

Check your manuscript for words and phrases that don't add anything to the sentence. For example: *a considerable amount, a bit, a little, slightly, somewhat, sort of, to a certain extent, a total of, approximately, close to, exactly, kind of, mostly, nearly, pretty* (when used as an adverb, as in *pretty spectacular*), *just, practically, quite, rather, really, simply, somehow, utterly, very, well.*

Here are a few more examples:

That. This word can often be eliminated without changing the meaning or flow of a sentence. But don't take out every *that* you find. If this little word improves flow or clarity, keep it. Not sure? Read the sentence out loud.

Actual/actually, honest/honestly, true/truly. If something you write isn't actual, honest, or true, you shouldn't be writing it. If it is actual, honest, and true, you don't have to say that it is. For example: "It's true that this bothers me, but I honestly don't know what to do about it." Better: "This bothers me, but I don't know what to do about it."

Suddenly. This word is unnecessary if what you describe happening would occur in a sudden manner. It's better to make suddenness clear from the text than to tack on this adverb.

Next and *Then.* These words are usually unnecessary because whatever you're about to describe happened after whatever you described previously. Sometimes, however, they do improve the flow.

Different. For example: "I sent three different manuscripts to five different agents, who submitted to ten different publishing houses." Take out *different* and the meaning remains the same.

So. If you say that a person or thing is *so* something (so hot, so beautiful, so amazing), you need to follow that by specifying what reaction that adjective caused. For example, don't write, "He was so handsome." Grammatically, you'd have to write something like "He was so handsome, my knees buckled." Unless this is a line of dialogue spoken by a character who would naturally talk that way.

Unnecessary Modifiers

While you don't need to delete every adjective and adverb in your manuscript, many can be eliminated without changing the meaning, especially if you use strong nouns and verbs.

Adverbs

Many adverbs end in *ly*. Find them easily by doing a search for "ly."

Best-selling author Gayle Roper says:

Search for *ly* and rewrite until most adverbs are gone. Don't do away with all adverbs, though. They are a valuable tool for writers. It's their overuse that presents a problem.

A strong, precise verb is almost always better than a weak verb paired with an adverb. Replace verb/adverb phrases with single-action verbs wherever possible. For example, you could replace "walked slowly" with *stalked, straggled, ambled, strolled, wandered, lumbered, padded, plodded, trudged.* Or "walked quickly" with *barreled, bustled, darted, hurried, jogged, raced, ran, scurried, sprinted.* Each word carries a slightly different connotation.

Sometimes, though, it's okay for a character to simply *walk.*

Best-selling author Gail Gaymer Martin says:

Instead of using adverbs (for example, "He said loudly"), select the most dynamic verb possible. He bellowed. He yelled. He screamed. He roared. He hollered.

Often, a better choice than using synonyms for *said* is to show emotions through dialogue and actions. For example, rather than telling readers "She screamed," write a scene that shows the character's fear or anger building. When you get to the line of dialogue, readers will know she screamed—because they'll feel like screaming too.

Redundant Modifiers

Eliminate adverbs and adjectives that don't add anything new. For example:

whispered *softly*

shouted *loudly*

terrible tragedy

reconsider *again*

future prospects

past history

completely finished

true facts

unexpected surprise

Excessive Modifiers

Don't use too many adjectives or adverbs, especially all at once. Readers don't need to know that the chair was a two-foot-wide wing-backed recliner with brown-and-tan checkered upholstery, 1970s style, made with coarse fabric. If all of those details are important, spread them out and weave them into actions and thoughts. Show the character collapsing onto the two-foot-wide recliner and running her hands over the brown-and-tan-checkered upholstery. Reveal memories of her childhood, back in the 1970s when her parents bought the chair, and how the coarse fabric scratched her little legs. Back then she'd felt dwarfed by the huge wing-backed monstrosity. Now she's resting her head comfortably on the high headrest.

Don't use more than two adjectives or adverbs together. For example: "The cold, gray, sterile, hard concrete walls closed in on Jack, making him feel lost, hopeless, helpless, buried, lonely, alone, and abandoned." Too many modifiers will make the reader think you couldn't decide on the right word, so you threw in a bunch. Instead, choose one or two of the most relevant ones.

Don't use two words that have similar meanings. For example, instead of "She struggled with deep, intense feelings and emotions of anger and wrath," choose deep *or* intense, feelings *or* emotions, anger *or* wrath.

Multi-word Phrases

In many cases, multiple-word phrases can easily be replaced with single words. Here are some examples:

at this point in time (*now*)

due to the fact that (*because*)

have an expectation *(expect)*

in the near future *(soon)*

it is clear that *(clearly)*

make an arrangement *(arrange)*

made the decision *(decided)*

in spite of the fact that *(although)*

has a tendency *(tends)*

in the event that *(if)*

with regard to *(regarding* or *about)*

And my personal favorite: pouring down rain outside. If there's *pouring,* it's probably rain, coming down, and outside ... unless you're a speculative-fiction author and weather works differently in your story world.

Action Delays (aka Filtering)

Rather than write that someone "began to" or "started to" do something, show him or her *doing* it.

Instead of telling the possible, show the actual.

Filtered: "He *could* sense that nobody believed him."
Better: "He *sensed* nobody believed him."

Rather than have a character "reach out and touch" someone, just have her touch. The reach is understood.

Instead of "He *decided* to leave," write "He left" ... unless he decided to leave and then didn't.

Rabbit Trails

For nonfiction, when giving examples of your points, be certain every illustration ties in to the main point of the section, the chapter, and ultimately, the book.

For fiction, don't let your characters spout off about topics that may be important to you, the author, but don't have a specific purpose in the story.

Don't Overcut

While tightening will make your manuscript more enjoyable for your readers, don't strip your writing to the bare bones. If you cut too much, the resulting dry, lifeless writing will bore your readers. Balance is key.

Read on a Device

If you have trouble focusing on the overall content of your manuscript because you can't stop yourself from being distracted by every typo, punctuation error, or misspelled word your eye catches, try reading what you've written on an electronic device.

Best-selling author Kathi Macias says:

Ever since I discovered I could send Word docs to my Kindle, I have made a practice of doing that with my editing projects. As I read them on Kindle, I look for things like continuity, content—any sort of potential macro-editing issues—leaving line editing to be done on my computer later. I am such a compulsive nitpicker that this is the only way I can focus on macro issues without getting sidetracked on minor issues and proofreading.

Chapter 7

EDITING NONFICTION

We've looked at several tips for editing nonfiction in previous chapters. But here we'll take a more in-depth look at editing suggestions specific to nonfiction. If that's your genre of choice, this chapter is for you.

Identify Your Genre

Nonfiction comes in a variety of genres. Here are some examples:

- Narrative Nonfiction (aka Creative Nonfiction)—information based on fact, presented in story format using fiction-writing techniques. Narrative nonfiction includes:

    o autobiography (the history of a person's life written by that person or told to a ghostwriter)

    o biography (a written account of another person's life)

    o memoir (story of a portion of a person's life, focusing on a specific theme)

    o short true story

    o travelogue

- Journalistic Nonfiction—a short essay or article that reflects the author's outlook or viewpoint on a particular theme or subject.

- Informational Nonfiction—text that provides facts about a particular topic. For example:

o   academic/textbook

o   business/finance

o   cookbook

o   cultural/social issues

o   gift book

o   health/fitness

o   history

o   how-to

o   humor

o   philosophy/religion/spirituality

- Bible study

- Christian living

- devotional

- theological

o   reference

o   self-help/self-improvement

o   technical (guide, handbook, manual)

o   travel

Determining which genre and subgenre your book falls into—or which it *should* fall into—is crucial since the style of writing is different for each one. After you've chosen the genre you believe fits what you've written, read numerous books in that genre and study the format, style, and tone as well as what's included and how it's included. Also read books about how to write in that particular genre. Then apply those techniques to your manuscript.

Of course, there is room for the individual author's creativity, uniqueness, and personality. However, readers who enjoy a particular genre will be accustomed to that format, style, and tone. They may be put off by something that's too different from what they're used to.

Weave in Anecdotes

Your nonfiction can come alive for readers if you use anecdotes to illustrate your points. These can be snippets from your own experiences, examples from the lives of people you know, or well-known, true stories of famous people.

Fictionalized accounts can be used to illustrate experiences that are common to many people. For example, "Sally looked for love in all the wrong places. But Fred was so focused on his business, he barely acknowledged her existence." Use common names (John and Mary, for example) or make up fun names (Foolish Fred, Silly Sally), depending on your target audience and the overall tone of your book.

If your manuscript doesn't include any anecdotes, consider whether or where you could add some. If you have included anecdotes, look at all of them individually. Does each one represent the point you're making at that juncture in the book?

If you use a lot of personal anecdotes, organize them chronologically. You may confuse readers if you describe something that happened when your son was a toddler in chapter 1, when he was a teenager in chapter 3, and when he was in elementary school in chapter 6.

If the anecdote is more than a sentence or two, use names rather than only pronouns or generic descriptions. Repeating "my best friend from high school" every time you reference someone will annoy your readers, and using *he* or *she* too often can be confusing.

Common Problems

Check your manuscript for these problems, which I see often in the nonfiction work I edit:

Rambling Introductions

Most new authors spend too much time at the beginning talking about their background, credentials, or personal experiences and/or explaining why they wrote this book. Your reader will lose interest if you don't quickly get to the reason they bought the book.

Establish the topic right away. Don't spend a lot of time describing how you found out about a problem, or how you talked to five people to get your information, or how your family and friends (or God) encouraged you to write a book. Get to the point as soon as possible, and pack the body of your manuscript with information too useful to delete.

Explaining "Why" but not "How"

A book that points out the importance of doing something without explaining how to do it leaves the reader thinking, *Okay, you've convinced me, but now what?*

Limit the "why" part to the introduction. Then give the reader steps for solving the problem you've established.

Not Asking the Right Questions

Even experienced writers can fall short of a reader's expectations by failing to ask and answer the right questions—specifically, the questions a reader is most likely to ask about the subject on which you've chosen to write. Often, this is due to the writer's closeness to the topic. Remember what you were like when you didn't know anything about the topic. In addition to writing about what you know, try to figure out what your readers don't know but want and need to learn.

Put yourself in the reader's shoes. Find someone who knows less about the topic than you do, and ask that person what he or she would want to learn about your subject.

Preachiness

Your readers want to know how to solve a problem or deal with an issue in their lives. But they don't want to be lectured. As a writer, it's your responsibility to inform or educate your readers. Leave preaching to the pastors.

To avoid preachiness in your manuscript, watch for the following.

- **Absolutes.** *Always never, everyone, no one, best, worst,* and other superlatives will put your readers on the defensive. Their natural reaction may be to respond with something like *Oh, yeah? Well, that doesn't apply to me. At least not all the time.*

- **Presumptions.** Don't claim to know what your reader is thinking or feeling. Check your manuscript for phrases such as "You're probably thinking ..." or "When you read that, I'll bet you wondered ..."

- **Imperatives.** It's tempting, once you've learned a lesson about something, to tell others what they *have* to do to get the same results you did. But readers don't want to be told what they must/need to/should/ought to do or not do. That puts them on the defensive. Here are some alternatives:

  1. Qualify your statements. "If you desire healthier relationships, try ..."

  2. Let readers know what they *can* do. What are the benefits of doing or not doing something?

  3. Share with readers what you've observed. Explain what you experienced, what you did, what happened as a result, and what you learned. Describe what worked and didn't work for you. Then let your readers come to their own conclusions about how to apply those lessons to their lives.

4. Reveal the research you've done. Let the reader know what legitimate, original studies have shown. Share the statistics you've discovered. (Make sure you properly cite sources for *all* statistics and studies you refer to.)

5. If you have to make "must" statements, use *we/us/our/ours* instead of *you, your,* and *yours,* which can come across as pushy. Using inclusive pronouns lets readers know you count yourself among those who need to heed the points you're making. For example, instead of "You need to spend more time with your family," you could write, "We could all benefit from spending more time with our families" or "Most of us have trouble finding time for our families." But don't use inclusive pronouns if the statement doesn't apply to you. That will come across as insincere or, at best, awkward.

Best-selling author Renae Brumbaugh Green says:

When offering advice or suggestions, make the problem about you, not the reader. Using the word *you* can sound preachy. If I set up the problem as my own, the reader sees me as transparent and gains wisdom from my errors.

Imagine how you'd speak to a close friend about these issues over a cup of coffee. Then imagine yourself as the listener and consider how you'd want to be spoken to.

Writing vs. Speaking: Know the Differences

Many speakers are asked to put their ideas into a book. But the written word is different from the spoken word. While maintaining the author's unique voice is imperative, a book should not sound like a transcribed speech.

Below are some of the ways in which writing is different from speaking.

Transitions

In a speech, it's easy to jump from one point to the next without much explanation. In writing, it's important for the reader to smoothly follow the author's train of thought. Transitions are required to make a connection between paragraphs, sections, and chapters. This gives the text a smooth, natural flow.

Repetition

Speakers often use repetition to help their listeners remember the main points. Reiterating information in creative ways makes the speech understandable and memorable.

Material presented in written form is retained better than when it is spoken. Readers can take notes and highlight the text for later review. They can go back and reread if they need a refresher. Therefore, redundancy can be frustrating. It can even be offensive or insulting if readers feel like you're talking down to them. *Does the author think I'm too stupid to remember what I just read?*

If you've said something once, don't say it again. Look for redundancy red flags like these in your manuscript:

- "As I said before ..." or "As stated previously ..."
- "As you will recall ..." or "As you may recall ..."
- "As we saw in chapter 3 ..."
- "To be clear, let me explain it a different way ..."
- "The point I'm trying to make ..."
- "In other words ..."
- "I want to make sure you understand ..."

Best-selling author Gail Gaymer Martin says:

Authors tend to fear that the reader didn't catch an important piece of information, so it is repeated over and over. I received a letter from a reader thanking me for not explaining everything more than once. It made her feel like I knew she had brains in her head.

Go through your manuscript with an eye for redundant words and phrases (besides "invisible" words like *the* and *said*), especially where they are repeated within close proximity. Consider where you can delete, reword, or rewrite a sentence to eliminate the repetition.

Step-by-Step Descriptions

Numbered or bulleted lists can build interest on a handout or in a PowerPoint presentation when detailed instructions are given verbally. But in written form they can look choppy or be confusing, especially if the explanations are lengthy. Instead, show the important steps creatively, with anecdotes and examples, and delete the obvious steps. Don't use more than four steps in a section or readers may have trouble following them.

Direct Questions to the Reader

Speakers engage their audiences by asking questions such as "Has this ever happened to you?" Listeners can respond verbally on the spot. While an occasional direct question may enhance a point in your book, too many can make you sound like you're quizzing your readers.

Wordiness

The following items can improve a speech, but they should not appear in a book.

- Preparatory clauses:

  "For my first point, I will show you ..."

  "The example I want to share is ..."

  "Allow me to explain ..."

  "Before I say something about ..."

  "Stay with me while I ..."

- Interjections (except in dialogue and only if used sparingly):

  "Whoa"

  "Yikes"

  "Hey"

  "Indeed"

  "Well"

- Opinion introductions:

  "In my opinion ..."

  "I believe/suspect/think that ..."

  "As far as I'm concerned ..."

Everything you're writing is your opinion, belief, or observation, so those phrases are unnecessary.

Use Facts and Statistics Properly

Don't pass along "facts" or "statistics" you've heard bandied about, or have read in someone else's writings, that don't contain the specific details that make a statistic valid and meaningful.

For example, how many times have you heard someone claim in a verbal speech that 50 percent of all marriages end in divorce? What does that mean? That half of all the marriages that have ever taken place, across the world, in the entire history of marriage, have already ended in divorce? That's not even possible.

Do your research. Find a reputable original source (*not* Wikipedia) for all of your facts and statistics, and include the specific information and details that apply to them. A legitimate statistic would read something like this:

> On March 22, 2012, the US Department of Health and Human Services published data from a 2006–2010 National Survey of Family Growth, in which 12,279 American woman and 10,403 men between the ages of fifteen and forty-four were surveyed. The 1995 NSFG showed that 50 percent of all women's first marriages ended in separation or divorce after twenty years. The 2002 NSFG showed that about one-third of men's first marriages ended in divorce after ten years.[6]

or

> In 2009, the national rate of divorce in the US was 9.7 per 1,000 for women aged fifteen and over, and 9.2 per thousand for men aged fifteen and over.[7]

Every statistic in your manuscript must be properly documented with a footnote (like the quotes above) or endnote (which would appear at the end of the chapter or the book).

Make sure you have cited your sources accurately. Check every word, spelling, punctuation mark, and capitalization. (For more on citing sources, see chapter 8.)

Portrayals and Perspectives

Does anything you've written in your manuscript reflect poorly on anyone besides yourself? If so, consider taking it out or rewording. In addition to legality issues (read more about that in chapter 8), do your readers really need to know all the dirty details about what someone else did? How would you feel if someone wrote that about you?

---

[6] Casey E. Copen, Kimberly Daniels, Jonathan Vespa, and William D. Mosher, "First Marriages in the United States: Data from the 2006–2010 National Survey of Family Growth," National Health Statistics Reports, March 22, 2012, http://www.cdc.gov/nchs/data/nhsr/nhsr049.pdf.
[7] Ibid.

Chapter 8

LEGAL ASPECTS

Various legalities come into play for writers. Traditional publishing houses are aware of literary laws, and they expect their authors to know about them ... and follow them. If you're self-publishing, you need to be aware of what the traditional publishers know.

If you have questions or concerns about any legal aspects of publishing your book, you may wish to consult a literary attorney—someone who specializes in the law as it pertains to the world of publication.

This chapter provides an overview of a few key areas.

Copyright Law[8]

Federal copyright law protects all "original works of authorship fixed in any tangible medium of expression from which they can be perceived, reproduced, or otherwise communicated."[9] Whenever a book, article, poem, drama, song, database, or illustration appears in tangible form—even if it's handwritten on a napkin—it is automatically covered by copyright, regardless of whether the work is published or registered with the copyright office. This protection lasts during the life of the author and for seventy years thereafter (for works created on or after January 1, 1978). Created works move into the public domain, where they are available for unlimited use by the public, when that time period ends.

When signing a contract with a publisher, the author guarantees that the submitted work is original and that no part of it has been

---

[8] Most of the information in this section was taken from copyright.gov.

[9] US Government Publishing Office, 17 U.S. Code Section 102, "Subject Matter of Copyright. In General," February 2016.

previously published or otherwise made public, with the following exceptions.

Creative Commons

Creative Commons is an American nonprofit organization whose goal is to increase the cultural, educational, and scientific content available to the public for free. CC licenses allow copyright holders to change their terms from the default of "all rights reserved" to "some rights reserved."[10]

If a work is licensed under Creative Commons, a notice to that effect will appear on the work as an alternative to the copyright symbol.

Commonly Known Facts

Accepted facts that could be verified by numerous sources (for example, "Abraham Lincoln was assassinated on April 14, 1865") do not need to be enclosed in quotation marks or given a source citation unless unusual or unique wording is taken directly from another work.

Fair Use

Fair use allows authors to quote limited portions of another author's work, even if the copyright holder has not given permission. No clear-cut rules specify how much leeway is allowed. Judges determine fair use on a case-by-case basis by balancing the following factors:[11]

1. **The purpose and character of the use**
   Educational purposes, such as making multiple copies for classroom use, are more acceptable than instances where monetary profit is anticipated, such as royalties from the sale of a book. Quoting a short section of someone else's work in your book to comment on or positively critique it is typically considered acceptable.

---

[10] https://creativecommons.org.
[11] See www.copyright.gov/fair-use/more-info.html.

2. **The nature of the copyrighted work**

   Courts favor the fair use of nonfiction more readily than fiction.

3. **The amount and substantiality of the portion used in relation to the work as a whole**

   Allowable quantity is evaluated relative to the length of the original and the amount needed to serve a proper objective. For example, copying an entire article would not be considered fair use. However, even short clips may be protected if they constitute the most extraordinary or creative elements of the piece.

4. **The effect of the use on the potential market for, or value of, the copyrighted work**

   Some courts consider this the most important factor. If your purpose is research or scholarship, market effect may not be an issue. If your purpose is commercial, market effect is presumed.

All four of the above factors must be considered when attempting to reach a responsible conclusion about the lawfulness of fair use. If you have any doubt, you should request written permission from the copyright owner prior to publication of your work.

The website of the publisher of the book you wish to quote from may include specific fair-use details for their authors' works. Thomas Nelson, for example, does not allow for *any* fair use of their books. All quotations, including excerpts from the Bibles they publish, require official permission, even for noncommercial use.

If you wish to use a significant portion of another person's material in your manuscript, you will need to obtain the copyright owner's permission, which sometimes means paying a fee. This fee is determined by the copyright holder and may be quite substantial. Most traditional publishing agreements stipulate that any fees to be paid for quoting copyrighted material are the author's responsibility. You will need to send the publisher all permissions you have obtained; these permissions will be filed with the publishing contract.

Even if what you want to quote is within fair-use guidelines, it's still a good idea to let authors know that you'd like to use quotes from their books in your manuscript. This can create good will, provide valuable networking, maybe even get you promoters or published authors to write endorsements or a foreword ... assuming they like the way you've used their quote. And if there's *any* question that they might not, you want to get permission up front, because they could cite you for violation of copyright law, even if the excerpt you've quoted is short.

Public Domain

When a copyright expires, the owner no longer has exclusive rights. Some authors and composers relinquish their copyright and give their material to the public, either during their lifetime or at their death.

The United States Copyright Office has published complex details regarding the provisions related to duration of copyright protection for published works. The term of copyright for a particular work depends on several factors, including whether it has been published, and, if so, the date of first publication. Here is a basic summary:

- For *unpublished* anonymous and pseudonymous works, and works made for hire, created before 1898, the copyright term is 120 years from the date the work was created (fixed in tangible form for the first time).

- Works published in the United States before January 1, 1923, can be assumed to be in the public domain.

- Works created between 1923 and 1977 are in public domain if they were published without a copyright notice.

- For works published between January 1, 1923, and January 1, 1978, published with a copyright notice or registered in unpublished form, copyright protection applies from the creation of the work. The original copyright lasts for twenty-eight years from the date it was secured, but the copyright may be renewed.

- For works created on or after January 1, 1978, copyright protection lasts for the life of the author plus seventy years.

For more detailed information on terms of copyright, consult chapter 3 of the Copyright Act,[12] Circular 15a, Duration of Copyright,[13] and Circular 1, Copyright Basics.[14]

You may use public domain material only if you have proof of public domain from a legitimate source. Seeing a quote in a book, on a list, or on a website is not sufficient proof.

The responsibility for determining whether a quote is in public domain, and obtaining permission if it is not, rests solely on the author's shoulders. This is not the duty of the publisher. However, both you and the publisher could be held liable for copyright infringement if you quote copyrighted material without permission.

You can search for copyright information about books, music, and other registered works at http://www.copyright.gov. Other legitimate sources for proof of public domain include the following:

- Original book or sheet music with PD (Public Domain) copyright date

- Photocopy of original book or sheet music with PD copyright date that you personally photocopied or was copied by a person or company you know and trust

- Digital copy of a book or sheet music with a PD copyright date printed from a CD or DVD published by a person or company you trust

Proof of public domain should include a copy of the original book's title page as well as the pages containing the material you wish to use. Keep this proof in your records for as long as your book is in print.

---

[12] https://www.copyright.gov/title17/92chap3.html.
[13] https://www.copyright.gov/circs/circ15a.pdf.
[14] https://www.copyright.gov/circs/circ15a.pdf.

No permission is necessary to use works in the public domain. However, acknowledgment of sources is still required.

Music and Poems

Other than private in-home listening and playing, fair use of music is extremely limited.

Titles of songs and poems may be used freely, as titles are not copyrightable. However, reprinting lyrics—even a few words—requires written and signed permission from the copyright holder ... unless it is in public domain. A short portion of a song or poem constitutes a far greater percentage of the whole piece than a brief quote from a book.

When doing public domain research, you must separately consider the status of each of the following:

- The music (the melody or the rhythmical sequence of single notes)

- The lyrics (words that are sung with the music)

- The arrangement (specific harmony notes played with the melody)

Most often, sheet music has a copyright date that includes all three. In some instances the music is in the public domain, but the lyrics are copyright protected. (See www.pdinfo.com.)

You may think that if you're self-publishing, no one will notice or care if you quote a few lyrics in your book. But music publishers are known to aggressively guard the content they have the rights to. If your book comes to their attention, they will very likely sue you for violation of copyright law. You could be forced to pay a hefty fine and destroy all unsold copies of your book.

Personal Communications

If you use stories from people you know in your manuscript, for a memoir or for anecdotes, get their permission first—and ask if they would prefer that you use pseudonyms and change identifying details. Show them what you've written, and the context in which you want to use it, and ask if they'd like to make any changes (or rescind their verbal permission).

If you use true stories of famous people, make sure you properly document and cite sources (unless it's common knowledge) and double-check your facts. But stories about non-celebrities could put you at risk of a lawsuit, even if what you write is accurate.

Anything someone tells you—verbally or in a letter, text, or email—belongs to that person, so you need his express permission to use it in your book.

Securing Permissions

Permission to use copyrighted materials must be obtained in writing from the individual or company that holds the copyright. When writing to request permission, include the following information:

- Title of the original work from which you are quoting and page number(s)

- Name of author/compiler/editor of that work

- Edition of the work, if other than the first

- Copyright date of the work

- Exact identification of what is to be reprinted

- Information about the book in which you wish to reproduce the material: title, your name, approximate number of printed pages, format of publication (hardcover book, paperback, journal, article, etc.), publisher, probable date of publication, approximate print run, and list price if available (Most of this information will be supplied by the publisher after the manuscript is under contract.)

- Type of rights requested (Your publisher will give you guidance on this matter.)

The person responding to your request needs to state clearly what fee is required for the proposed use and any special conditions that may apply. The copyright holder will either sign and return to you one copy of the request or will send you one copy of the copyright owner's standard form. A second copy of the permission form will be retained in the copyright owner's files. If you are working with a traditional publishing house, give the original to the publisher and keep a third copy for your reference.

When to Obtain Permissions

Permissions need to be sought as early as possible. Obtaining permissions may take months. Permission may be refused, or the fee may be too high for you to pay, in which case you will need to rewrite certain sections. Your book cannot be finalized until all permissions have been received.

If you have multiple quotes from a single source, you may wish to include a special mention in the acknowledgments section in the front or back matter of your published book. The copyright holder might have specific guidelines concerning the placement and phrasing of the credit line.

Cite Sources

Proper documentation gives credit to the original author, enables readers to locate the sources of your quotes, and lends credibility to your work. If you don't properly cite your sources, you are committing the crime of plagiarism.

You may find the same information on the internet, but that doesn't mean you can quote it in your book. On most websites, the originator isn't making money off the content, so it's not as important to quote the original source. With a book, you're probably planning to get paid for sales, and with an article, you're hoping to get paid by the publisher. Payment and publication are major factors in copyright law.

If you find an internet article that quotes another source, don't put that quote in your book without properly citing the original source of the quote, even if the website doesn't.

If you can't find out who initially came up with a quote or story, take it out of your manuscript.

Methods for Citing Sources

There are four main methods for documenting sources: footnotes, endnotes, a bibliography, and the copyright page.

- **Footnotes**

  References are cited in the text by superscript numbers ([12]).

  A footnote number should come at the end of a sentence, or at least at the end of a clause. The number *follows* a quotation and its punctuation, whether the quotation is short and runs into the text or long and set off from the text by block indenting. Occasionally it may be inserted after an author's name or after the text introducing the quotation.

- **Endnotes**

  Endnotes are typically placed at the back of a book, after any appendix material and before the bibliography, arranged by chapter. Or they may be placed at the end of each chapter.

  Most publishers prefer endnotes over footnotes if there are several notes in the book or if they would take up a significant amount of space on a page.

- **Bibliography**

  A list of books and other references used by the author may be placed at the end of the book, before the index. In a work containing many footnotes or endnotes, a bibliography in addition to the notes can be a useful device for the reader and an economical one for the author and publisher. Full particulars for each source need to appear only in the bibliography; citations in the notes may be shortened or abbreviated.

- **Copyright Page**
  If your manuscript contains quotations from the Bible, put a Scripture copyright notice in the front matter of your book for every version you quote from. Each Bible publisher has its own specifications for how many verses may be quoted without requesting written permission. So check the website of the publisher of the Bible(s) you have quoted from in your book. (This information is also available on BibleGateway. com.)

  The King James Version is in public domain in the United States, so there are no limitations to quoting from it (unless you are publishing outside the US). However, you must still identify the version on your copyright page.

Formatting

For detailed instructions on formatting endnotes, footnotes, and bibliographies, see the appropriate section in the most recent edition of *The Chicago Manual of Style.*

Chapter 9

EDITING MEMOIR

A memoir is different from an autobiography. Autobiographies are typically written about celebrities (people the general public has heard of and is interested in discovering details about), often telling the individual's full life history—the most interesting parts, at least. Memoirs, on the other hand, are snippets of a person's life that are all related to a specific theme. Memoirs are more popular than autobiographies if the author is someone readers have never heard of.

To edit your memoir effectively, follow these steps.

Step 1: Overall Analysis

Legalities

Before you go any further with your manuscript, check out the legal aspects of memoir writing. The following websites provide solid information and advice:

http://www.writersdigest.com/writing-articles/by-writing-goal/get-published-sell-my-work/defamation-and-invasion

http://helensedwick.com/how-to-use-real-people-in-your-writing/

http://www.rightsofwriters.com/2011/01/can-you-tell-your-own-true-story-even.html

http://writers.stackexchange.com/questions/8310/permission-requirements-from-people-in-my-memoir http://penandthepad.com/write-true-story-being-sued-5730056.html

If what you write could cause someone harm—even if it's true—that person could sue you for libel, defamation, invasion of privacy, or misrepresentation. If that individual is deceased, his or her family members/successors could sue you.

Changing names and locations is insufficient protection against a lawsuit. Every potential identifying detail would need to be altered. You'd have to write under a pseudonym and refrain from telling anyone you authored the memoir. Marketing or promoting the book will be extremely difficult without revealing your identity, which would in turn reveal the identity of everyone you mention in it.

Even if the people you write about don't sue you, how will they feel about you and behave toward you if you write these things about them—especially if you publish the book? How will you feel about yourself if something negative happens to those people as a result of your writing about them in this memoir? How would you respond if someone wrote such things about you or your loved ones?

If what you've written could potentially result in legal or moral issues, I urge you to reconsider your publishing plans.

Identify Your Motives

Ask yourself, *Why did I write this book?* Consider these valid purposes for writing a memoir:

- Catharsis (your personal healing from reliving past events)

- Legacy for family and friends (those alive now and future generations)

- Revealing the truth (as you see it)

- Telling others about what you've experienced

- Sharing what you've learned with those who may be going through similar experiences

- Honing your writing skills

Consider Your Target Audience

Once you know your real reasons for writing this manuscript, ask yourself who would benefit most from reading it.

If you're writing for your own catharsis, that can be very helpful for you. But is there a takeaway for someone else?

Will this story be of interest to anyone other than your family and friends? If you think it will intrigue others, determine your main target reader's age range, gender, marital status, religious background, and beliefs, etc. What about your story will appeal to that group of people?

Leaving a legacy for family and friends is delightful ... for you and for them. But will anyone you don't know care about what you've written?

Best-selling author Jerry Jenkins says:

When writing your memoir ... You may be the subject, but it's not about you—it's about what readers can gain from your story.[15]

Analyze Your Publication Plans

If your story will appeal predominantly to family and friends, you may wish to self-publish, which could mean printing or emailing copies of a PDF file or using a company that will format your print book or e-book and allow you or others to purchase copies online. With this option, the writing level is less important than if you hope to attract the attention of a traditional publishing house.

If you have a way of selling multiple copies of the book yourself, through speaking engagements or online marketing, you may

---

[15] Jerry Jenkins, "How to Write Your Memoir: A 4-Step Guide," https://jerryjenkins.com/how-to-write-a-memoir/.

choose to subsidy publish, which involves paying others to do what you cannot do, such as editing, proofreading, interior layout, and cover design. Or become your own publisher, which means doing everything a publishing house would do on your own. Either way, the writing will need to be more polished than if your target market is solely family and friends.

Best-selling author Cindy Sproles says:

Medium-sized houses will publish memoirs if the story is compelling and it's a topic that house has experience and success in tackling. Smaller houses will publish a well-written memoir, but their reach in the marketplace is very limited. Self-publishing puts a book out there, but more times than not, it's lost in the millions of books on Amazon. Unless the author has a steady speaking venue where books can sell at the back door, sales will be slim to none. Memoirs are rarely, if ever, money makers.[16]

If your goal is to make public something that others may want to keep secret, you're writing an exposé more than a memoir. Traditional publishers are unlikely to accept a tell-all book because it could get you and them into serious legal trouble. And will that really do anything positive for anyone?

Writing a memoir is an effective way to learn writing techniques. Some people have found that getting their own stories out of their hearts and minds and onto the page frees them to write other books and articles that are published later.

If your goal is to help people by sharing your life story, ask yourself how much detail from your past is truly necessary to accomplish that purpose. Focusing more on your personal healing

---

[16] Cindy K. Sproles, "The Good & the Bad about Writing Memoir," July 24, 2018, https://www.blueridgeconference.com/good-bad-memoir/.

will be far more beneficial to your readers than revealing and rehashing private specifics about the trauma.

If you want to help others, consider writing a genre other than memoir. Would the readers you're trying to reach be inclined to look for (and purchase) a true story about someone dealing with the same issues they're struggling with? Or would they be more likely to search for a book, article, or blog that shows them how to handle those problems? A how-to, inspirational, or devotional piece could include anecdotes from your past to illustrate your points, and those snippets are less likely to include details that could result in a lawsuit.

Consider Your Marketing Plans

As you think about the possibility of publishing your memoir, consider how you will market your book to your target audience.

If you're simply revealing what you've experienced in life, what will make people who don't know you want to read about it?

Sharing what you've learned with those who may be going through similar struggles in the hope that it will benefit them is an honorable goal. But will your genre choice of memoir reach and appeal to those readers?

Tighten Your Writing

You will be tempted to include certain details because they are exciting or important to you or because they feature someone who means a great deal to you. But if they aren't relevant to your theme, take them out.

≈≫⦂⊹⦂≪≈

Best-selling author Mona Hodgson says:

Only include things that will actually interest your reader and make them want more. So what if your cat hacked up a hairball? Just because something happened, that doesn't mean it's interesting.

≈≫⦂⊹⦂≪≈

Look for phrases such as "I remember ..." or "I can still recall ...." *Everything* in a memoir is something you remember, so that verbiage is superfluous.

Take out any inside jokes that only you and your family and friends will appreciate—unless they are your only target readers.

If your memoir includes references to a particular culture, important people or events in history, or details of careers or hobbies not your own, double-check your facts for accuracy. Errors, even minor ones, will undermine your credibility with your reader.

Step 2: Study

If you haven't already done so, read books about how to write, study tips on authors' and editors' websites, attend writers' classes, workshops, and/or conferences. (My list of recommended resources is in Appendix A.)

Read books, articles, and blog posts specifically on how to write a memoir.

Read popular, recently published memoirs and analyze them to see how the authors used specific writing techniques. Consider how you can incorporate those techniques into your memoir.

If you do not want to expend the time and effort to learn professional writing techniques, you may wish to hire a collaborator/ghostwriter to write your story for you. Expect to pay for the professional's time and expertise. You may also need to share the byline (*by* you, *with* the collaborator) on the book cover and/or title page. Unless you are a celebrity with guaranteed sales, a professional will not write your story solely in exchange for a promised split of potential royalties.

If you decide to hire a professional writer, follow as many of the other steps listed here first. The more you do yourself, the less the collaborator will have to do for you. This will not only save you money and save both of you frustration, but you'll be more likely to end up with a final manuscript you're happy with and proud of.

Step 3: In-Depth Edit

Once you know who your target audience is and what your publication and marketing plans are, you can determine what level of editing your book needs.

If you're writing about your life for personal healing, no one else is going to see it, except perhaps your therapist. So it doesn't make any difference whether you edit it.

If you want to share your life story as a legacy for family and friends, most of them won't care how polished your writing is. But you still want to make sure you've communicated clearly. Editing can help prevent your written words from being interpreted in ways you didn't intend.

If you're writing your memoir primarily to polish your writing skills, the process of editing it can help you develop your self-editing skills as well.

If you want to submit your book to a traditional publisher, the writing quality must be stellar. That's true in any genre, but especially memoir.

As you self-edit, consider the following aspects.

Theme

What is the specific theme of your memoir (for example, recovering from an eating disorder, dealing with an abusive spouse, handling the death of a loved one, or living with a chronic illness)? If you come up with multiple themes, you may have enough material for more than one book.

For now, pick one. Delete anything that does not relate to that chosen theme. Or move it to a folder for possible use in a future book.

Tone

Determine the overall voice of your memoir: conversational, informal, reserved, professional? Do you want the tone to be humorous, dire, cynical, optimistic, serious, sentimental?

Revise any material that doesn't fit your desired tone.

Order

Memoirs may be told chronologically (in the order in which events occurred) or in whatever order heightens the impact. Just make sure the story flows smoothly, without too much jumping around, which can confuse the reader.

Step 4: Use Fiction-Writing Techniques

Although a memoir is based on true events, it should read like a story. The most interesting parts should be shown (described in active scenes) rather than told in straight narrative ("This happened and then that and then this").

Read the chapters of this book on editing fiction and study the techniques discussed there. Below is an overview of how they apply to memoir writing:

Point of View

Your memoir should be written in first person—you telling readers about what happened to you. Don't include any details you could not have known at the time each part of your story took place.

If you wish, you may tell stories from your past as a present-time narrator. For example, "I enjoy a wonderful relationship with my father now, but that hasn't always been the case." As the narrative moves into the past, use a transition to put readers into the story. For example, "When I was a teenager ..." Stay in your perspective at that time in your life. Save further reflections for after you've moved out of the past story and returned to the present with another transition. For example, "Those turbulent adolescent years are behind me now."

Characters

In real life, we encounter many people who play a small part in our lives for a limited period of time. In a written story, even a true one, the appearance and disappearance of minor characters can be disconcerting for readers. Which individuals have had the most impact on that part of your life? Don't include people simply because they're important to you ... or because you think they'll be disappointed if they're not mentioned in your book.

Each person in your story needs to be interesting to your readers, so weave in enough detail about all of them, and include them in enough scenes, so your reader gets to know them and like them—or at least understand them.

If you choose to include people who have identical or similar names, consider how to differentiate them to avoid reader confusion.

Scenes

Considering your memoir's chosen theme and your target audience, decide which parts of your life would make interesting active scenes. For cohesiveness, one scene should lead naturally to the next— unlike real life. This isn't lying or being untrue to what actually happened. It's an effective storytelling technique. As long as you accurately portray the essence of what happened, you're being faithful to reality.

Each scene should revolve around a particular conflict. If everything is going smoothly, that won't be interesting to your reader. For every scene, ask yourself: *What did I want? Why did I want it so badly? What was stopping me from getting it? What was I willing to do to achieve my goals? What did I attempt to do? How did that work out for me?*

Backstory

Don't start with a dramatic opening scene and then leave that scene to fill in a lot of information about the events that led up to it. Weave in carefully chosen details in bits and pieces as they become important to the reader's understanding of what's happening in the current scene.

Description

Include brief descriptions of people and places. Provide enough details for readers to visualize, but avoid superfluous bits of minutia that don't relate specifically to the story.

Dialogue

Dialogue makes a scene come alive and gives readers insight into how people communicated with each other. It also reveals personalities and moods. The words don't need to be a precise transcript of everything that was said, just a truthful reflection that is authentic and relevant to your story.

Show, Don't Tell

In the scenes you've written, look for places where you identified emotions. Instead, describe the situation with enough sensory detail that readers will *feel* how you felt. If you reveal your thoughts along with what you were doing and observing, you won't have to tell readers what emotions you experienced.

For example, let's say your father left the family when you were young. You could tell readers you were sad and then angry. But that won't make them feel sad or angry for you. Instead, reflect on a crucial moment in your childhood. Think about what led up to it and what happened—and then describe that incident in a detailed scene.

Show your parents fighting—again. To get away from the yelling, you escape to the garage and hop on your bike for a trip around the neighborhood. As you ride, you sneak glimpses inside windows of other homes and see families hugging and laughing. With eyes blurred by tears, you pedal harder. You reach a small hill. The bike goes faster than you can control. It veers into a hedge, knocking you off and skinning your knees and elbows. As you pick up the bike, you notice the front tire has gone flat and the chain is loose. You limp home, dragging the bike beside you. Mom's car is no longer in the driveway. When you walk through the front door, you find Dad sitting in his favorite worn recliner, his eyes red. He stands when he sees you, and you're sure you hear him sniffle. You show him the bike. He kneels beside you and examines it. He tells you he's going to get you a new chain and a new tire. And then everything will be okay. Swiping his cheek with the back of his hand, he stands and walks out the door. That's the last time you saw your father.

Add in some description and dialogue (using the techniques covered in the fiction editing section of this book), and that scene will elicit strong emotions in your reader—without you once telling how you felt.

Plotting

A good story has a beginning, a middle, and an end.

The beginning shows the "main character" (you, the memoir narrator) involved in a conflict of some kind, doing something interesting. Consider where you've started your story. Will that opening scene, even the opening paragraph, hook readers and make them eager to find out what happens next? Does the chapter end with a scene that will compel them to read on?

The middle of the book shows how you attempted to resolve the initial conflict and all the ensuing conflicts. It reveals your goals and the obstacles to those goals, as well as how you attempted to reach those goals and overcome the obstacles. Every chapter should end with a hint of more conflict to come, to keep readers turning pages.

A good story occasionally surprises readers. If your memoir is predictable, readers will get bored and stop reading.

Everything in the manuscript should progressively lead toward a powerful moment in which it seems impossible for you to achieve your desires. The most intense point in the story, the decisive moment that creates a major turning point in the plot, is called the climax. It should come near the end of the book.

The last few pages should show how you either reached the goal you established in the beginning or realized that you were better off going a different direction. How your memoir ends is as important as how it begins. While real life never gets tied up in tidy bows, the memoir needs a satisfying resolution. What message do you want readers to come away with after reading your story? Make sure that message is clearly communicated by the end. Don't leave your readers hanging, but don't draw out the resolution either.

Step 5: Share

Show the manuscript—or at least relevant parts of it—to anyone involved in or connected to each scene or the full story. Even if what you wrote reflects them in a positive light, contact everyone you've written about who could possibly be identified by themselves or others and obtain written, signed permission to use their information, life history, and names in the memoir.

Then give the manuscript to people who don't know you or your story well. These people represent your target audience. Ask them to read your manuscript and give their honest impressions—both what they liked and what they think could be improved.

Finally, share your manuscript with other memoir writers, and/ or a professional freelance editor who specializes in memoir, to get feedback on how to make it even better. (See chapter 19.)

Chapter 10

EDITING FICTION— INTRODUCTION

I've given a few tips for editing fiction in previous chapters. Now let's take a closer look at some aspects of editing related specifically to fiction. These techniques will help make your novel a page-turner ... and possibly a best seller.

Before we start, let me offer a bit of advice. When you're talking with a professional in the publishing industry, or writing a query letter, one-sheet, or book proposal for an agent or acquisitions editor, never use the phrase *fiction novel.* A novel is, by definition, fictional. Adding the redundant adjective will make you seem like an amateur.

Following is a checklist that was adapted from a variety of sources, including the Hartline Literary Agency website (http:// www.hartlineliterary.com/submit.html), best-selling author Deborah Raney's adaptation of that information, and guidelines established by a group of judges at a large writing contest. These are the most common reasons fiction manuscripts are either considered or rejected by agents and traditional publishing houses.

Originality

Do some market research. What other novels out there are like yours? How is yours different? This doesn't mean tried-and-true plot devices can't be used. But they need to be implemented in a fresh way that piques the interest of the publisher—and eventually readers.

Page-One Hook

Does your story open with a scene that will capture a modern reader's interest? Is your opening line captivating enough to make people want to read on? Will the first page entice them to turn to the second page?

Hook at the End of Chapter One

Your first chapter should end with a cliffhanger. This is true for all of your chapters, but especially the opening one.

Likable Protagonist

Your main character should not be *all* good. If he's a person of virtue, albeit slightly flawed, the reader will enjoy finding out what happens to him. If he's an unlikable person, or acts in ways your readers disapprove of, they won't care about him. They might even want him to get the punishment he deserves.

Redeeming Qualities in the Antagonist

Just like your protagonist shouldn't be all good, your villains shouldn't be all bad. They must have a clear, understandable motivation for their actions. In real life, most people don't consider themselves bad. They know why they do what they do, and it makes sense to them.

Appropriate Point-of-View Characters

Is the POV character for each scene wisely chosen and easily identified at the beginning of every scene? Are the transitions from one perspective to another smooth and necessary?

Good Supporting Characters

Are your secondary characters believable, realistic, and interesting? Is each one a valid addition to the story? If not, take him out.

Clear Goals

Your main character must have a well-defined goal that is vital to his existence—perhaps to the existence of several people. He must be willing to do *anything* to accomplish his goal. Of course, that goal must not be accomplished—at least not without page after page of obstacles to overcome, and preferably *not* in the way the character or reader anticipated.

Tension and Conflict

Your characters' goals must be diametrically opposed to each other. Each person must encounter seemingly insurmountable obstacles. Start with small-stakes conflicts that gradually become more crucial. If the opening scene is too intense, you won't have anywhere to build to.

Realistic Dialogue

Does the dialogue sound natural and realistic? Does it build characterization and move the story forward?

Balance of Dialogue and Narrative

If your manuscript consists of almost all dialogue, with a few actions and speaker attributions thrown in, you're writing a script, not a novel. Plays and movies rely on what the characters do and say to communicate with the audience. In a novel, you can weave in the POV character's thoughts and observations to create a richer experience. Fiction readers want to get into the minds of the main characters, to live the story through them, not read *about* what happens to them.

Pacing

Readers will want to keep turning pages if the pacing flows well throughout the book. Don't put a fight scene or argument on every page. Good pacing is a balanced combination of action and reflection.

Descriptions

Are the time and place established at the beginning of every scene? Is the location easy to picture without taking over the story? Have you provided enough details for readers to visualize what your characters look like? Have you shown details of people and places from the POV character's perspective?

Overriding Theme

Your book should have a specific purpose. Don't spell it out in an obvious fashion, but don't hide it so well that your readers miss it. At some point in the story, give your main character an aha moment, when she suddenly realizes something important about herself, about someone else, or about life.

Style and Voice

Every author has a unique writing style. It may take a while for you to discover your voice, but you don't have to work at it. Simply write in a way that comes naturally to you, and in time you will develop a style that people who know you will recognize when they read your writing.

Note, however, that ignoring the industry-standard rules for punctuation, usage, grammar, and spelling is *not* a matter of style or voice. Nor is choosing not to follow well-established guidelines for writing fiction. That's just laziness or stubbornness.

Going Deeper

Some of these concepts might be unfamiliar to you. Or you may have heard the terms but aren't sure you fully understand them. In the following chapters, we'll delve more deeply into the various aspects of editing fiction.

Chapter 11

EDITING FICTION—PLOTTING

*P*lot is what your characters do during the course of the story. Some novels are action oriented (plot driven), while others are relationship oriented (character driven). But even in relationship-oriented novels, the characters must *do* something.

Beginning

Don't start with flowery descriptions of setting or a flashback of the character's history. Begin with *action, adventure, intrigue, suspense.* The reader should know what the story is about in the first twenty to forty *lines*, not pages.

The best way to start a story is to *show the main character, with an immediate problem, doing something interesting.* Involve the reader quickly with this character, arouse curiosity, and give the casual browser who picks up your book the feeling that he or she *must* know more about what this character is doing and why.

Begin with a conflict situation that is typical of the main character's normal life—before whatever happens to turn his life upside down and set him off on a quest, journey, or adventure.

Don't let your main character be alone with his thoughts. Include one or two major secondary characters in the opening scene to provide interaction. This will enable your reader to get to know your important characters and relate to them right away. But don't introduce too many characters in the first chapter, or your reader will have a hard time keeping everyone straight and remembering who they all are.

Introduce your hero, heroine, and villain within the first few chapters. Show their unique personalities through what they do and say—and, if they're POV characters, what they think.

Your characters' actions should be connected to their wants, needs, and goals. What are they trying to achieve? The stakes don't have to be life-or-death. Something small, like winning an argument or getting a kid home from the grocery store before a tantrum starts, can work great—if that sets the tone for the book and helps readers understand your characters.

The main character's heartfelt goals, the ones she'll try desperately to accomplish during the course of the novel, should be clearly revealed in the first one or two chapters. You don't need to reveal all the reasons these goals are important to her happiness. But there should be some hints right up front, with more detail gradually revealed as the story progresses.

Inciting Incident

Toward the end of the first chapter, show the *inciting incident*—what happens that changes the character's normal world and previous life direction. What new goals arise as a result of this incident, and what obstacles stand in the way of accomplishing those goals?

You may be tempted to start your story with a bang (literal or figurative). But beginning with a high-action or deeply emotional sequence where your main character's life or heart is at stake won't be effective if your readers aren't connected enough with that character to care what happens to him.

Starting with a scene that occurs right *before* the inciting incident, as he struggles with a conflict that typifies his normal life, allows readers to get a feel for his personality and character traits. Make him likable, relatable. Then, when that crisis occurs, readers will feel his angst and root for him to overcome it.

Middle

The middle of your novel consists of scenes that reveal pivotal information about the characters' background and internal conflicts. Do those details come out naturally? Are the characters *doing* something that brings out these revelations?

Your main character needs a *purpose*—and that purpose must be opposed in nearly every scene. What actions does your main character take to overcome the obstacles you've placed in his path?

During the course of the story, the main characters need to change, for better or worse. This change should happen gradually, realistically. Examine your characters one at a time, looking for the progressive steps in their transformations.

Every chapter, scene, and line of dialogue must advance the plot in some way. If you find one that doesn't, chop it out.

Conflict and Tension

Tension keeps readers turning pages. And to have tension, you must have conflict. Make sure you've included plenty of conflict in each scene: thwarted goals, formidable obstacles, powerful enemies.

The main character's goal should have a time limit for completion. A sense of urgency will heighten the suspense. This writing technique is known as the "ticking clock." It could be a literal timepiece, such as a timer on a bomb, or some kind of deadline that must be met to avoid doom, failure, or loss of the important dream or goal. The deadline should be believable and intrinsic to the story, not arbitrary or self-imposed by the protagonist.

Raising conflict, defeating your character's purposes, and blocking the accomplishment of goals can become depressing if it goes on too long. High tension that never lets up can become as monotonous as no tension at all.

Sometimes, after a struggle, the main character's purpose may appear to succeed, providing hope that he'll reach the ultimate goal. Then more trouble comes. The final answer to the struggle isn't reached until the end of the novel.

Some temporary relief along the way offers a small reprieve from the building tension, a chance for the reader to breathe. But even in quiet scenes, your main character should still have a *problem*, a *purpose*, and a *goal*.

Flashbacks and Backstory

Avoid flashbacks during the first thirty to fifty pages of your book, when you're trying to get your readers involved in the action, conflict, and suspense of the present story. Resist the urge to explain the background of your characters, thinking readers need to know all that information to understand what's going on. Instead, show what happens, and save the explanations for later, when you can weave them into the story in ways that don't detract from the action.

Best-selling author Gail Gaymer Martin says:

One common error is an author's belief that paragraphs of backstory must be shared for the reader to understand the story. Bring the characters to life with action, let the reader see the character's goal or need, provide conflict, and show some of the character's mannerisms. In little spurts, and only when necessary, add pieces of backstory that will enhance the impact of the story.

When you come across a flashback in your manuscript, ask yourself if that part of the character's past is vital to the story at that point. If the same information could be presented in dialogue or woven into the narrative, do that instead.

When you choose to keep a flashback scene, don't let a character spend an entire page reminiscing about the past, either in thought or dialogue. If you've captured your readers' attention, they'll want to move forward and find out what happens next. Yes, they'll be somewhat interested in why the characters are doing what they're doing. But they want those details sprinkled in throughout the story so it doesn't come to a screeching halt for a few pages.

Revealing hints of a character's background as the story continues will whet the readers' appetite to know more. A vague allusion to a tragic event in his past will pique their interest and make them wonder what really happened. This adds to their desire to read on, so they can find out more details about something you've hinted at. Each time you reveal one more piece of the puzzle, you rev up the readers' desire to discover more.

Best-selling novelist Lori Freeland illustrates how to effectively weave pieces of background information into an active scene with this paragraph from a current work-in-progress:

> Up until today, my sister hadn't said much about my Josh addiction. Not last summer, when I started lying to Dad. Not last fall, when I slid homework into the optional category. Not even last month, when I walked away from my position as captain of the cheer squad.

Lori says, "In the short paragraph above, you get a sliver of backstory on who this girl used to be (honest, good student, involved in activities) compared to who she is now (a liar, an apathetic student, isolated from others) and the reason for that change (her new boyfriend)."

Here's a second example:

> "Yes, ma'am." Alek's smirk went pure Texan, and he moved in to put his arm around me.
>
> A chill broke over my skin. My recently acquired auto-flinch didn't care that my best friend had hugged me a thousand times before. It overrode every single time we'd squeezed into a crowded booth in a restaurant, shared a cushion on the couch, and fallen asleep against each other while movie-marathoning in the game room.

Lori comments, "Her reaction to Alek trying to hug her shows their past relationship and leaves readers wanting to know what changed and why."

Using Flashbacks Effectively

Flashbacks can be an effective tool when used properly and judiciously. When they're not written well, or if they're overused, they can stall the pace, interrupt the flow, or even bore the reader. So analyze every flashback in your manuscript. Is it truly necessary? If so, is it written in a way that will enhance, not detract from, the plot?

If you have a compelling reason to keep a flashback scene, follow these steps to take the reader smoothly and seamlessly from current action to memories of the past and back again.

- Build up to the flashback by foreshadowing it. Weave snippets into the dialogue and/or narrative that allude to something in the character's past. Make the reader curious about the details. Then, when your reader is *dying* to know what happened, reveal the backstory in an appropriately placed flashback.

- Stay in the point-of-view of the character who has the flashback. A person's thoughts cannot be observed by someone else—unless that someone else is a mind reader!

- Put your character in a position where his mind would naturally wander. If someone is pointing a gun at the hero's temple and saying, "Give me your wallet," a thought may flit through his mind, but he won't stand there musing for several paragraphs about something that happened years ago. He's going to react! Later, when he has collapsed on the concrete and is leaning against the building, shaking from head to toe, he could have a flashback. But even that should be interrupted by another action before the musings go on for too long.

- Have something trigger the memory you want to show. Was your character in that same hospital waiting room when she was told her best friend died? Does she find a photo album in the attic that brings back memories?

- There must be conflict within a flashback. The tension in the flashback should increase the building tension in the current scene.

- When you're ready to transition into the flashback, use phrases that let the reader know you're going back in time. Something like "He remembered that moment like it happened yesterday." Or "Joe stared at the run-down baseball field. The last time he'd seen it ..."

- Start the flashback scene with verb tenses including *had* and *had been* for a sentence or two, then move into simple past tense. Here's an example, with the transition verbs in bold:

  Michelle **had been** a shy teenager at the time. She**'d** worn oversized glasses, and her face was riddled with acne. When the cute boy in fifth grade said, "You're pretty," her heart raced. When he added, "Pretty ugly," and sauntered away laughing, she wanted to crawl into a tunnel and never come out.

  The beginning transition verbs set the scene in the past. Details reveal how far in the past.

- When you're ready to move back into current events, use another transition. Make it as smooth and subtle as your opening transition, gently bringing your reader back to the time, place, and actions of the current scene. Use words that will remind the reader of what was happening right before the flashback started.

  For example, following the previous flashback, you could write:

  As she stood in front of the bathroom mirror, she realized why the hottest guy in the office had asked her out this morning. She was now—dare she think it?—pretty.

  You may use a sudden interruption of the character's thoughts to get out of a flashback. For example, "The sound of a slamming door jarred Melanie from her memories."

Ending

The conclusion of your story should have five distinct parts: *crisis, black period, awakening, climax,* and *resolution.* Read your final chapters and identify each of these parts.

The *crisis* is the section where everything goes devastatingly wrong for the main characters. The challenges and obstacles they've faced have grown steadily worse throughout the story. Their failure seems complete and irreversible. They will never reach their goal. All is lost.

This hopeless situation leads to the *black period,* where the main character comes to the lowest point of discouragement in his mind and heart. In a romance, the hero and heroine are separated— if not physically, at least emotionally and/or spiritually.

Then comes the *awakening*—the point where one or both main characters realize that a fear needs to be faced and conquered, a goal needs to be changed or forgotten, the love relationship can work *if* he/she does ... whatever suits your plot.

This leads to the *climax,* the scene where the main character puts it all on the line one last time. He goes for broke, holding nothing back. And it works!

In the *resolution,* the main character has achieved his big goal— either the original one or a revised, better one. He learned something along the way that made him a better person. He has changed in the process, and he's pleased with his new-and-improved self.

If your final chapter connects to something in the opening chapter, your story will have a satisfying "bookends" feel.

Timeline

Create a chapter summary for your book. For every scene in each chapter, identify the POV character, location, day of the week and date, and a brief description of what happens in that scene. You don't need to include all of these details in the manuscript. But it's important for you to know what happens at each point in the story.

Highlight each POV character in a different color. This will help you see whether too much time has passed between each character's appearance in the story. It will also identify any random scenes that are shown from the perspective of a character who isn't a POV character. Those will need to be rewritten from the perspective of one of the POV characters.

Review the dates on that timeline. Do you have any places where more or less than seven days of activity occurred in the course of a single week? Too many or too few days in a month?

In what seasons do your scenes occur? Does your character notice the weather? If a chapter takes place in the middle of a Midwestern winter and your character goes outside or looks out the window, make a brief mention of the temperature or how much snow is on the ground.

Where do major holidays and other significant events land in the course of your story? Does your character celebrate Christmas, his birthday, New Year's Eve, Valentine's Day? Does he at least notice other people celebrating, or preparing to celebrate, those special days? If he doesn't celebrate them, how does he feel about that?

If you have a Mother's Day scene, followed by several things happening, then have your character celebrate Father's Day, make sure you have exactly four weeks of activities between the two holidays.

Wherever something important happens to the character that has lasting ramifications, have you shown those ramifications? For example, if a character has a car accident, do you mention whether he took his vehicle in for repairs or dent removal and whether insurance covered it? Does he have symptoms of whiplash—or worse?

Look for story threads that come up in one scene but aren't followed up. For example, if a character twists her ankle, make sure to mention the next time that character appears in the story how her ankle feels, if she needed a bandage or a cast or crutches, or whether she walks with a limp.

Look for characters that come up in one chapter and aren't mentioned again for several more chapters. If too much time lapses between a character's appearances, add a scene so the reader doesn't forget about that person.

Look for dropped story threads, then pick them up and tie them off.

Chapter 12

EDITING FICTION—CHARACTERS

For fictional characters to seem like real people, they need physical characteristics. Male or female. Tall or short. Thin or fat. Eyes, hair, feet, and hands—or something different if they're not human beings!

But characters need more than bodies. They need a life—past and present. They have friends and enemies. Likes and dislikes. Strong opinions. Like people in the real world, their actions typically reflect their personalities—but characters can also act in unpredictable ways.

To determine how your characters would act, speak, and think in a given situation, you need to know them intimately. Where have they lived and worked? What kind of childhood did they have? Who broke their hearts? Who has mentored them? What excites them? What do they fear most? The answers to these questions will influence the way they talk and behave within your story.

Use a thesaurus to collect a few adjectives, adverbs, nouns, and verbs that accurately describe each character. Don't try to give all the details. A few highlights will suffice.

You may wish to gather pictures from print or online magazines, advertisements, or catalogs to help you envision your characters. Or consider what actor would best suit each main character in your story and find a photo of him or her. Look for images of clothing and jewelry your character might wear, places your character may visit often, such as rooms in their homes. Put these pictures in a folder on your computer or in a three-ring binder, with separate sections for each of your characters.

Copy every description that appears in your manuscript and paste it into a computer file so you can keep all the details straight and make sure they're consistent.

Personalities

When you introduce your characters, their actions should reflect their personalities. Give your readers hints as to who they are, what they want, what/who they care about. What is their purpose in life? Show these insights through their actions, their words, and their choices.

Next, think about your characters' personalities. What are their goals? What are their professions and hobbies, virtues and vices? What do they care about? Are they happy? Fearful? Sarcastic? Lonely? Bitter? Self-assured? Timid? What do they like/dislike?

What are your characters' flaws?

Best-selling author Gail Gaymer Martin says:

New authors often create good-looking heroes and heroines. They have sunshine for picnics, avoid characters' bad habits, and make most everything pleasant. The problem is, positive and nice lacks realism, and it doesn't encourage conflict.

Sadness, shame, irritating habits, and ordinary looks are real. Novels will offer more to readers if they can learn how "not so perfect" people discover that life can still be beautiful.

Add rainstorms to a picnic, make the heroine's hips broader than she wants, create a hero who drums his fingernails on tabletops, and have the first date be a bust. Then allow characters to work toward change, to make a bad situation better, and find fun in unwanted situations.

What are your characters' secrets? And how do those secrets come to light in the story? If you reveal details gradually, your reader will anticipate finding out new information as the story progresses.

What are your characters' motivations? Have you revealed enough for readers to understand them?

Best-selling author Lena Nelson Dooley says:

Every action, reaction, or word spoken must have a motivation. Examine everything any character in the book does, then ask yourself, "Why did he or she do that?" If you can't answer that question, take the word or action out, or build in more of a motivation for it to happen.

Emotions

What feelings do your characters experience during the story? We all go through a range of emotions every day. Having characters experience multiple feelings makes them seem more real to your readers.

To understand your main characters' emotions more completely, try writing in a diary as if you were one of those characters. Of course, these entries would not be included, word for word, in your novel. But as your character "talks" about himself in the first person, he may begin to feel more real to you. You may be surprised to learn what he thinks, especially about the other characters in your story.

Some authors like to interview their main characters, asking them questions and jotting down how they think the characters would respond.

Quirks

To make your characters realistic, give them idiosyncrasies.

Best-selling author Gail Gaymer Martin says:

People are not always rational or perfect. They can step outside their values, morals, and beliefs and do things they never dreamed they would. They don't always see themselves or their surroundings with clear eyes. Handsome men don't always know they're handsome. Women with lovely bodies are sometimes bulimic because they think they are fat.

Consider the irrational qualities of real people and give some of your characters peculiarities. These qualities can create unique, interesting characters and/or powerful conflicts in your novel.

Character Sketches

Create a detailed character sketch for each of your main characters. Include every physical attribute mentioned, either in narrative or dialogue. If your hero has blue eyes in chapter 1 and brown eyes in chapter 8, fix that inconsistency—unless you made this change for a reason and made it obvious to your readers.

Write down every detail of your character's life that comes up more than once. Then confirm that everything in your manuscript is consistent, including the spelling of your characters' names.

Here is a sample list. You may not have something in each category for every character. But if a detail is mentioned in the manuscript, it should appear in this file.

Name

Full name, nickname(s), aliases (including maiden name)

Connections to Other Characters in the Story

Friend, best friend, mom, mentor, follower

Purpose in the Story

What unique role does this character play? How is the main character affected by this character? If you can't come up with an answer, consider taking the character out of the story.

Physical Description

Gender, age, height/weight/build, health, race/ethnicity/ citizenship, hair color, hair length/style, eye color, complexion (fair, dark, freckled, tans/sunburns easily), facial features, facial hair, hands/fingers/fingernails, posture/stance, walk, speech, visible marks or scars, impairments/disabilities, any distinguishing characteristics

Current Life

Home (location and description), own or rent
　　Who lives with him, marital status (for how long)
　　Car (or other mode of transportation used)
　　Pets (current and past and/or hoped for)

Past

Where and when born, where lived, jobs held, dreams accomplished, crushed, or abandoned
　　Previous jobs, relationships, marriages, military involvement
　　Biggest regret, most humiliating experience, most triumphant experience, dark secret(s), favorite memory, greatest heartache

Family

Give names and describe the relationships between the character and his or her spouse, parents (still married or divorced, and for how long), siblings (older or younger by how many years), children (ages), aunts, uncles, cousins, stepfamily.

Current Relationships

Friends, enemies, romantic interest, conflict with romantic interest (what keeps them apart), dangers if they get together, benefits if they get together, relationships with other protagonists, relationships with antagonists

Education

Grade school/high school/college, adult/continuing education, special training, extracurricular activities, sports

Business

Job/occupation, place of employment, position, long-term career, current success level and satisfaction level, financial status

Favorites

Color, drink, food, dessert, book/genre/author, movie/TV show, actor/actress/celebrity, season, pastime, spectator sport/game, participation sport/game, sports team

Psychological

Attitude, mannerisms, habits, manner of dress (clothes, jewelry, accessories), neuroses, hobbies, talents/skills, quirks/idiosyncrasies

Spiritual

Religious beliefs (what and why), denominational affiliation, religious activities (what, where, and how regular), significant spiritual experiences, spiritual gifts

Values

What does your character value? (Some examples: money, status, reputation, security, loyalty, resourcefulness, honesty.) Values tend to stem from upbringing, so they're typically deep-seated and not easily changed.

Personality

Personality type/temperament

Greatest strength, greatest flaw. Does he recognize his own strengths and weaknesses?

How do others see him? How does he see himself?

If he could change one thing in his life, what would it be?

Top priority, greatest need or want, long-range goal/dream, short-range goal(s), deepest longing, deepest fear. (What's the worst tragedy that could happen to your character? Make it happen!)

Spend some time with the Personality section. If you don't have a good feel for your character, research personality types. Imagining yourself as the character, take a personality quiz, and answer the questions as she would. Then score the test to see what her type is.

Read the detailed description of the personality type and see if it matches how you perceive your character, including what careers that kind of person is drawn to. If it's not a good fit, you may have some misunderstandings to clear up. If it is a good fit, you'll learn even more about your character as you study those details.

Look also at the charts that show which personality types get along best together and which have the most conflict. A protagonist and antagonist with opposing personality types will generate additional tension.

Changes during the Story

For each of your main characters, ask yourself:

How do his strengths overcome his weaknesses or cause him problems?

How do his weaknesses prove to be strengths or get him out of trouble?

What new strength(s) does he gain along the way?

What does he learn by the end of the story?

How does he change by the end?

How do other characters change because of their interaction with him?

Best-selling author Susan Meissner says:

Every good novel presents the reader with a character who wants something and must overcome opposition to have it. The emotional glue of a story is that the reader identifies with what the character wants and why.

The *why* is what bonds readers to the main character and entices them to keep turning pages. If they don't know why the main character wants something, it won't matter whether or not she gets it. And if they don't care whether she gets what she wants, they are going to put down the book.

As you approach the editing stage of your novel, solidify your main character's motivation by asking, *Why does this character want what she wants?* Keep asking that until you know her better than you know yourself.

Does your character's deepest motivation show up in the pages? If not, make a list of all the places in the book where you can go back and show it. Identify the places that are most organically tied to the plot and your character's main goal, then weave in details that reveal the why of it all.

Chapter 13

EDITING FICTION—
POINT OF VIEW

Point of view is a writing technique readers rarely notice but publishers and professional authors are keenly aware of. If POV isn't handled properly, readers may sense that something doesn't feel right, even though they can't pinpoint what's wrong. Errors in point of view will brand a writer as an amateur to a publisher, and no matter how good the story may be, it will probably never be traditionally published—or successfully self-published.

"Point of view" refers to the perspective (or perspectives) from which the reader watches the story unfold. The point-of-view character is the "consciousness" of the story. The reader sees, hears, smells, tastes, and experiences everything that happens through that character's perceptions.

Point-of-View Options

Below is a brief explanation of the most common POV alternatives.

Omniscient

In the omniscient point of view, the author oversees the story from a distance, revealing the perceptions of his characters when he deems it necessary or helpful. You will find this technique in many classic novels, but it is not popular in modern ones.

The omniscient voice distances readers from the story because it cannot convey a deep sense of a character's growth through the course of the book. Personalities are revealed by telling the reader what the characters are like, rather than showing. This puts readers

110 Editing Secrets of Best-Selling Authors

at arm's length, never close enough to any character to become emotionally involved in his life.

The omniscient viewpoint is very different from the readers' personal experience. In real life, you can't see what's going on in the next room. You can't know what will happen ten years from now, or even tomorrow. When a novel is written in omniscient POV, the reader will have more difficulty believing the story is possible.

Writing in the omniscient point of view is tricky. Only the most gifted, experienced authors can use it successfully.

First Person

With this option, a narrator tells the story by using first-person statements ("I said this; we did that"). All events are observed through the narrator's perspective and must be consistent with what he thinks, knows, and believes. Detective novels are often in first person, with the narrative written in the voice of the main character.

Autobiographies and memoirs are typically written in first person, which can create a natural, conversational style. First-person POV may also make a fictional story more personal and seem more real. However, it carries some challenges and limitations:

- Attributing negative aspects to a narrator's personality is difficult. Since people don't typically see their own faults, narrators often end up appearing even-tempered, friendly, kind, thoughtful, considerate—and boring.

- You can't conceal information from the reader that the narrator knows.

- You can't reveal information that the narrator doesn't know.

- Excessive repetition of "I" can distract the reader from the story.

- Readers may feel uncomfortable relating intimately with a character who acts in ways they consider offensive or objectionable.

Seasoned authors can sometimes make a first-person story work. However, new writers should not attempt this technique.

Second Person

Second-person POV is most commonly used when describing a process, giving instructions or advice, providing information, or writing personal correspondence. A story told by a character referred to as "you" usually comes across as intrusive and irritating, so novelists don't use it.

Third Person Singular

The most prevalent form of contemporary fiction—and the preferred option for new writers—is third person ("She said this; he did that").

In a singular third-person narrative, the entire story is told from one character's perspective. The point-of-view character must be present, awake, and conscious in all of his scenes, and everything is experienced through his senses. The character's thoughts are revealed using his own words. Other characters' thoughts, feelings, and personalities are displayed through their dialogue and actions, as perceived by the POV character.

Having one POV character limits you to only what that individual can know and observe happening. It makes the story linear, which can get monotonous.

Third Person Multiple

Most novels tell their stories through the emotions, thoughts, and desires of two or more major characters. When done well, this technique involves the reader emotionally with all of the POV characters.

Romance novels are always written from two points of view. About two-thirds of the story is told from the heroine's POV, the rest from the hero's. For other genres, it's best to have from two to five point-of-view characters. If you have too many POV characters, readers will have trouble keeping track of who's who. If you try to tell the whole story from one character's perspective, you'll be limited in how much you can show.

The first POV character mentioned in your book's first chapter should be the main character, the individual through whom most of the story will be lived. Introduce each of your main characters within the first few chapters, and don't let too many chapters go by before the reader is back in each character's perspective.

Once you've chosen who your POV characters will be, determine which character's perspective is best for each scene. Who will be able to observe everything you want to portray? Who has the most to gain or lose from the outcome of that scene? Who will be most affected? Who will have the deepest level of emotional investment and internal conflict?

Switching between POV characters adds tension. Suspense is heightened when you leave one character's storyline hanging to show what's happening with another character. You're showing an active scene filled with conflict, and you end the scene with a hook, filling your reader with anticipation. She turns to the next chapter or gets past the scene break, and instead of finding out what happens next, she is thrown into a different plotline from another POV character's perspective, filled with different tension. She will have to wait a scene or two, maybe a chapter or two, to find out how that previous conflict will be resolved. This is what creates page-turning fiction.

Making the Choice

Consider the POV choice you've made in your manuscript. If you feel constrained by the limitations of that option, try a different one and see if you like it better.

Once you've chosen a POV option, be consistent throughout the manuscript. For example, if you're writing in third-person point of view, beware of second-person statements in the narrative.

Incorrect: When they asked for directions, the answer was so confusing that you could never find your way.

Correct: When they asked for directions, the answer was so confusing that they could never find their way.

Editing for Point of View

Each scene needs to be shown from one character's perspective. If you want to switch from one character's POV to another, either start a new chapter or insert a *scene break*—a blank line with a single centered pound sign (#) or three asterisks (***).

The first character mentioned after a chapter or scene break, or the subject of the first sentence, is considered the POV character for that scene.

A chapter or scene break can indicate a change in point-of-view character, location, and/or time. Therefore, at the beginning of every chapter and scene, make sure you've clearly established the following:

- *who* the POV character is and who else is there

- *what* is happening

- *where* the scene occurs

- *when* the scene takes place (but not "the next morning" or "three days later," as that's not what the POV character would be thinking at that moment)

- *how* the POV character feels about the situation (without telling readers what emotion he is experiencing)

Look at the beginning of every chapter and scene in your book. Do the first few sentences make it clear who the POV character is for that scene?

Go through the entire scene and make sure you've shown what the POV character is thinking, observing, sensing, and feeling.

Best-selling author Lori Freeland says:

Don't fortune-tell. Example: "If Jim had only known the meat was spoiled, he never would've made it his late-night snack." Unless Jim is psychic, he isn't going to know that the decision he made today will ruin his tomorrow ... and neither can the reader.

Look through your manuscript for places where you've shown what other characters are thinking, feeling, or observing—which the POV character could not know. He might be able to guess what those around him are thinking or feeling based on what they do or how they look. But you need to describe other characters exclusively through the eyes of the point-of-view character.

Best-selling author Lena Nelson Dooley says:

You can grab a reader and not let go by pulling that person into the deep places most characters like to wall off and not approach. Only in those hidden places can we really get to know the person.

Read your manuscript and see how much depth you have in these areas:

- Secret desires—good or bad

- Secret hurts—the ones they've never told anyone

- Secret plans—fun or devious

Then go through the manuscript and mark places where you could add even more of these layers.

Give the reader glimpses of those secret places at first, and deeper glimpses as you go along, until some upheaval reveals the depth of those places near the end of the book.

Deep POV

In a technique known as deep POV, you write narrative directly from the mind of your POV character, removing filter words—the author's comments on what's happening. Deep POV enables readers to make a stronger emotional connection with the characters, taking the journey of the story along with them.

Best-selling author Eva Marie Everson says:

Instead of telling what a POV character experienced ("She saw a car drive by"), show what happened ("A car drove by"). That puts the reader into the action. Then enhance it with the emotion that went along with the action. ("A car drove by. The same make and model, even the same color. Had he found her?")

Wherever you've written that a character *thought, believed, wondered, noticed, saw, felt, knew,* or *decided* something, take those words out and simply show what was thought, observed, or felt. A character doesn't think those words, so they shouldn't appear in the narrative.

Here's an example from best-selling author Lori Freeland of a first-draft paragraph from her novel *The Accidental Boyfriend* (with filters and "telling" words in bold):

I grip Gabriel's arm tighter. But my fingers tingle. They **feel** numb. Even when I flex them. **My throat closes. I see and hear** everything around me fading, and I can't decide what to do. **I wonder** if I should run away or just close my eyes and pretend I'm not even here.

Strong hands grab my waist, keeping me upright, but inside **I feel** cold, and **my ears roar**. **I feel** my chest get tight. And **I think** I might pass out.

Here's her revised version in deeper POV, without the filters and with more showing:

I grip Gabriel's arm tighter. My fingers tingle. Go numb. Stay numb. Even when I flex them. Cotton expands in my throat. Everything around me fades into a dull kaleidoscope. The room shrinks, my world shutting down. My body can't decide whether to float away or compress into lead.

Strong hands grab my waist, keeping me upright, but inside I tumble into ice-cold panic. A rushing river fills my ears, swallowing all the sound. Invisible fingers fist inside my chest, squeezing. Smothering my heart. Muffling the sluggish beat. Dissolving, disintegrating, I sink into myself, like I'm being vacuum-sealed from the inside out.

The first version distances the reader from the action. The revised section pulls readers into the POV character's head and heart.

Here's another section of Lori's first-draft version from that same book:

If Gabe hugs me tighter, I'll suffocate. But **I know** I need to be there for him. **I decide** to stay in his arms, the whole time **wondering** what I can say to make him feel better about his mom being here. **I search my mind** for the right words and end up rubbing my cheek against his chest. When he tips his head, **I feel** wetness on my neck. **He's crying.**

And his silent tears **make me sad**. I know how it feels to lose someone.

Here's the revised version, in deeper POV:

> If Gabe hugs me any tighter, I won't be able to breathe.
>
> But I don't want to forfeit my chance to be his lifeline. So I stand on the walkway in front of the memory-care center, desperate to say something, anything, to make him feel better.
>
> Nothing I say will change his mom being here. So in place of worthless words, I press my cheek against the rapid pulsing of his heart.
>
> When he buries his face in my neck, dampness touches my skin. His silent tears scrape me raw. I know how it feels to have your life ripped from you. To suffocate in the restless ache of losing someone *who's still here.*

Internal Discourse

Internal discourse (aka internal monologue) is what your POV characters think but don't say out loud, either to themselves or to other characters.

Only the POV character in a particular scene can have internal thoughts.

If you're writing in third-person past tense, and you show a character's thoughts in first-person present tense, those words should be in italics. For example:

> She fanned herself. *I just want to cry.*

You could rewrite the sentence to eliminate the italicized first-person, present-tense thoughts.

> She fanned herself, desperate to cry.

For deeper POV, you could write the character's direct thoughts without first-person, present-tense wording.

> She fanned herself. Don't cry.

Best-selling author Lori Freeland says:

Internal discourse can serve a variety of functions.

- It allows you to show readers how your POV character feels.

Trace startles me enough that I jump. He might be two inches shorter than Cade, but he makes up for it in ego.

- You can use internal discourse to set a mood.

It didn't help that I was alone in a house that was more "modern mausoleum" than "contemporary living."

- Use internal discourse to weave in backstory or character relationships.

"You're not driving in Dallas traffic." Dad wouldn't notice if I *played* in traffic.

- Internal discourse can build tension.

"What are you doing here?" Don's expression changed from bored to lethal.

I felt the color drain from my face all the way to my feet. Don had killed Lisa. And now we were alone.

- Internal discourse can make a potentially unlikable character likable by revealing his motivation.

"Didn't ask for your help. Don't want it." I shut him down with a quick cut of my voice. When he hung his head and shuffled away, I was the one who bled.

Give each of your characters a unique internal voice that sets him or her apart. Make sure it matches the details of your character: gender, age, background, etc.

Best-selling author Lori Freeland says:

Amplify dialogue by supporting, expanding, or contradicting dialogue. Here are examples of each:

- Supporting dialogue:

  "That's not possible." It's an excuse he'll believe.

- Expanding dialogue:

  "You can't just call him." It's like an unwritten law or something.

- Contradicting dialogue:

  "It's fine." It's not fine. But Dad doesn't do labor intensive.

Avoid long paragraphs of internal thought, especially in the middle of a tense scene. Instead, weave the character's thoughts into the action and dialogue so readers can know what he's thinking while things are happening.

Chapter 14

EDITING FICTION— SCENE, SEQUEL, AND SUMMARY

The most powerful stories have a good mix of scene, sequel, and summary.

Scene

Scenes are told in real time. Readers vicariously experience events as they happen, rather than hearing about them after the fact.

Scenes have specific *locations,* physical *action, dialogue,* and *narrative*—all of which must be woven together. Too much description in one long chunk can kill suspense and interest. Too much dialogue without narrative, and your characters' conversations will seem to go on forever. Too much narrative, and your readers will feel stuck inside the characters' heads.

Each scene should include one or more of the following:

- new information about one or more of the characters that is pertinent to the story

- aspects of setting that affect the characters or plot

- events that advance the storyline

A scene that accomplishes all three of these purposes is ideal. Any scene that does not accomplish at least one should be deleted.

Best-selling author Randy Ingermanson says:

A scene has the following three-part pattern:
1. Goal
2. Conflict
3. Disaster[17]

A *goal* is what the POV character wants to achieve. *Conflict* is what stops the hero or heroine from easily achieving the goal. *Disaster* results when the character fails to reach his goal. If characters get what they what, there's no reason to continue. A disaster motivates readers to turn the page.

Make sure all of your scenes flow smoothly from one to the next. Don't give your readers what I call "literary whiplash" by jumping from one time, place, or point of view to another too often or too suddenly. If you need to change time, place, or point of view, insert a chapter break or scene break to alert the reader.

Sequel

Readers can't be on a constant adrenaline high. Sequels give them a chance to catch their breath before the next action-packed, conflict-laden scene. Randy Ingermanson says, "A sequel has the following three-part pattern: reaction, dilemma, decision."

Reaction. When disaster strikes, your POV character will respond to it.

Dilemma. The reaction leads to a dilemma: the POV character is left with no good options.

---

[17] Randy Ingermanson, "Writing the Perfect Scene," https://www.advancedfictionwriting.com/articles/writing-the-perfect-scene/.

Decision. Your POV character chooses the best possible option under the circumstances. This becomes the goal for the next scene.[18]

Dwight Swain coined the term MRU (Motivation-Reaction-Units) for this process.

Motivation is what happens to your point-of-view character that makes him want to do something.

Reaction is what that POV character does in response to the motivation. This may include action, dialogue, thoughts, or emotions.

A Motivation-Reaction Unit is comprised of (a) something that motivates the POV character, followed by (b) the character reacting by doing, saying, thinking, or feeling something. This reaction can lead to a new motivation.

Identify the MRUs in each of your sequels. If you find any motivations without reactions, or reactions without motivations, add the missing element.

Summary

Summary is used to cover spans of time and to provide an overall description of events that are less important than events described in scenes.

If an event in your story involves only minor characters, or repetitious actions, or small talk, summarize it. If you have a minor event that leads up to a key scene, summarize the first event so the scene, when it comes, will seem more immediate by contrast.

If any scene in your rough draft does not move the plot forward, summarize it or delete it.

---

[18] Ibid.

Best-selling author James Scott Bell says:

Show the intense scenes and tell the less important transitions (the narrative summary) between important scenes. As a guide, if what you are writing has the possibility of present-moment dialogue, it is a scene. If not, you're in summary.

Chapter 15

EDITING FICTION— SHOW, DON'T TELL

A cardinal rule for fiction writers is "show, don't tell." More than anything else, this technique can bring your story to life and make your readers feel like your characters are real people they actually know.

Emotions

When you want readers to know that a character is feeling a particular emotion, don't *tell* the reader how she feels. Instead, *show* that emotion through actions, body language, and/or facial expressions.

For example, instead of telling readers, "She was depressed," show her eating an entire carton of cherry-cheesecake ice cream in one sitting. Or maybe she sits at the table, a double-fudge chocolate cake in front of her, and she can't force herself to eat a single bite. Or she picks up the cake—which she spent an hour frosting—and throws it in the trash.

To indicate romantic attraction, don't tell the reader, "She felt strangely attracted to him." Instead, show her noticing the hair on his chest or the fullness of his lips. Show how she reacts when his hand brushes against hers as they reach for the saltshaker at the same time.

Crying, weeping, sobbing—pretty much anything to do with tears—can be improved if you create a sad scene or situation and show the character's thoughts about it in such a way that your reader feels the sorrow. Then you won't have to tell readers about tears.

Best-selling author Gail Gaymer Martin says:

Is there anywhere in your manuscript that you "told" the readers something you wanted them to know that doesn't come across as a natural part of the story? Instead of telling readers how a character feels ("She was excited"), show that emotion through actions. ("She jumped out of her chair, threw her arms around her father's neck, and covered his stubbly cheek with kisses.")

Next time you watch a movie, look for ways the characters reveal their emotions without words. One of the best examples I've seen (I don't remember where I saw it, or I'd give credit for it) was a scene where some people were in an emergency room waiting to hear whether their loved one had survived a surgery. Some people paced, others smoked, one yelled at the kids, another sat in the corner staring into space. Finally, a surgeon walked down the hall toward the family. His stride was purposeful, his eyes focused on the floor. He pulled the surgeon's cap off his head, gripped it in his hand, and flung it to the ground with a scowl. Everyone in the room—and in the audience—knew the patient had died. Yet not a single word was spoken.

Best-selling author Lena Nelson Dooley says:

Emotions and motivations are closely related and often overlap. But we need to see the emotion—in internal thoughts or as observed by the POV character if another character is experiencing the emotion. With the POV character, include visceral reactions and external reactions. Show how what's happening reveals itself in the POV character's body—sweaty hands, burning in chest, churning stomach. But use creative ways to express it—ways that fit with that character's past and present.

Levels of emotion can be revealed more clearly by showing than by telling. If a character is perturbed, she might grit her teeth. Furious, kick a cabinet. Enraged, throw something across the room. A more specific degree of anger can be revealed by the choice of object thrown—the more fragile, expensive, rare, or sentimental it is, the more anger is revealed. The object may represent something symbolic, such as Kevin Spacey's character in *American Beauty* throwing a dinner plate full of food his wife had prepared.

Best-selling author Gail Gaymer Martin says:

In place of "I felt sick," show how the character felt through more vivid language. "Nausea roiled in my stomach, burning its way to my throat with the stench of the decaying body." This sentence is far more dramatic and makes an impact on the reader.

Creative ways of *showing* emotions will make your characters seem more real, will enable your readers to visualize what your characters are doing, and will attract the attention of a publisher or agent.

Dialogue

Don't *tell* the reader how a character's dialogue sounds. *Show* it instead. For example, "She said with disgust" *tells* the reader how a line is spoken. Instead, *show* the emotion with actions. She could curl her lip, place her hands on her hips, or look down her nose at the person she finds disgusting. Rather than write, "She said shyly," *show* her shyness with actions. Have her dig her toe in the dirt, lower her eyes, or finger the hem of her blouse.

You may think that having a character use profanity shows emotion. However, this tactic can be an indication of lazy writing. If you take the time, you can probably come up with words that convey even more intensity than swearing.

Curse words in print can be offensive to readers, even for people who are used to hearing those words in movies or everyday life. Rather than risk losing a percentage of your readership, *show* a character's emotions with actions.

If it is imperative to let the reader know that a character uses profanity, find creative ways to do so. "He swore," for example. Or "He let loose a string of epithets that made her face turn crimson." This has the added advantage of showing another character's reaction to the swearing.

In one novel I read, a TV reporter was trying to get a rude, nasty man to talk to her on camera. He yelled at her. The author wrote something like this: "His crude remark won Julie boatloads of sympathy with her audience." Do we know what was actually said? No. But readers can fill in their cusswords of choice—or choose not to.

Background

If you show a woman in a bright-colored sports jacket putting an Open House sign in a yard, you don't need to tell readers she sells real estate. If you show a character taking apart a complex electronic device and putting it back together properly, you don't need to tell readers he's an engineer.

Look for places in your manuscript where you've told readers something about your characters that could better be shown by what your characters does and says.

Best-selling author Eva Marie Everson says:

In my edits, I look for those times when I tell the reader what the character feels, both with her skin and with her heart. In place of "I felt nervous," I write, "My heart hammered and my leg, which I failed to steady, bounced like a basketball at the end of a dribble."

Wherever the word *had* appears, you're likely telling readers what *had* happened instead of showing something happening in the present. You may occasionally want to provide some backstory or insert a brief flashback. But those times should be few and spaced out. So when you see the word *had,* ask yourself if it would be better to show that information in an active scene.

Don't Show Everything

There are instances when what happens in a story should be told—when it's not crucial to the plot and/or not terribly interesting. That's called summary. (See chapter 14.) If a character needs to move from one time or place to another, don't show every step. Just tell readers where he went.

Show and Tell

If you've *shown* something, don't *tell* the reader too. For example, if you show snow on the ground, you don't need to have your character say, "Brrrr. It's cold out here."

Once one character has revealed something, don't have another character say the same thing. And if you've shown a character doing something, don't spend the next few pages having that character tell other people what happened in detail.

Best-selling author Gail Gaymer Martin says:

If a character has an experience, and then has a phone call, don't have the character retell what happened to another character. Instead, use a summary transition, such as "After telling Joe what she'd seen, Allie pulled up her shoulders and waited for his response." Or, "Forming the awful words in her mind, she related the horrible situation to Joe." Now the author can move along with new information—a discussion about what happened or possible solutions to the problem. Or, if you're in the other character's POV, you can show that character's response to the situation.

Chapter 16

EDITING FICTION— DESCRIPTIONS

Readers need to visualize the characters and settings in a novel. Descriptive details enable them to see in their minds what you've imagined in yours. However, too many random details can bog down the story.

Character Descriptions

As each character enters a scene, provide a creative description of that character's physical appearance. Keep it brief, related to the action, and in the point-of-view character's perspective. Use details that enhance the mood, character, and plot. What does the heroine notice about the hero when she sees him for the first time? What does she notice about him after she's spent a few weeks getting to know him?

Replace flat descriptions with action as much as possible. Instead of writing "John was tall, with black hair and brown eyes, and he wore a hat," try something like this:

> John ducked slightly as he entered the room. When he noticed Mary standing in the corner, he removed his Seattle Mariners cap, revealing a mop of thick black hair that stuck out in every direction. His dark eyes darted back and forth as if he expected a wildcat to lunge at him. Mary stared at the long fingers of his left hand as they squeezed the cap and realized he wasn't wearing a ring.

Vary your descriptions. For example, don't describe each character's clothing every time one of them enters a scene ... unless the point-of-view character's personality revolves around clothing—perhaps she's a fashion designer, so clothing is something she would notice.

Showing the appearance of your point-of-view character can be tricky since she can't see herself. Using a mirror works occasionally, but this method can seem contrived, especially if she doesn't have a good *reason* to be looking in a mirror and if you don't show what she *thinks* about her appearance.

Be careful not to describe attributes of the POV character that he or she would not be able to observe. For example, "Debra's cheeks reddened." If Debra is the POV character, she can't see the color of her own cheeks. She could, however, feel her cheeks grow warm.

If a character's clothing reveals something about her problem, her personality, or her mood, describe it when she does something with it. Don't tell the reader what she's wearing. Show her adjusting her wire-rimmed glasses, pulling down her short denim skirt, wrapping her thick gray sweater more tightly around her body. Use actions that show the reader how the character is feeling.

Setting

Create visual images that not only show where the action takes place but also reveal something about the characters and the story.

The right setting can add depth to characters and their relationships, set a particular mood, and even serve as an allegory for your characters' emotions.

Setting description is far more than the name of a town, the size of a room, or the location of a restaurant or park. It can include details such as the weather, season, month, year, and time of day. If a scene takes place outdoors, show something about the weather and how it affects the POV character and those around him.

Does your manuscript have long paragraphs filled with adjectives that tell what a location looks like? That will bore your readers and take them out of the story. Instead, weave the pertinent details subtly into a scene, always from the point-of-view character's perspective.

Envision the room's décor. Is it cozy, formal, drab, cheerful, elegant? Is it sparsely furnished or filled with knickknacks? Such elements reflect the room's owner and provide clues to that character's personality.

Describing the setting in which your action takes place allows the reader to visualize the scene through the perceptions of the point-of-view character. Do this unobtrusively, without overwhelming the scene or interrupting the story. Too little detail leaves your characters wandering around an empty stage. Too much, and your readers will be tempted to skim.

Some novels depend on a particular setting to create suspense or danger. Scenes that depict descriptive details of a location prepare the reader for a future incident or situation that applies to that setting. For example, a deserted mountain cabin, miles away from the nearest neighbor, would be vital to a story about someone trapped by a killer, snowbound by a blizzard, or injured and in need of rescue. Weave enough detail into each scene so the reader can visualize where the action takes place, but not so much that the reader is distracted from the storyline.

In real life, we explore our surroundings through our *actions, experiences, moods,* and *senses.* The same should be true in your writing.

Actions

Instead of writing, "A heavy oak table dominated the room," show your character walking around it. Instead of explaining that "light shone from the crystal chandelier," show your character blinking at its brightness. Break the details into bite-sized nuggets scattered throughout the scene.

Experiences

Different characters will perceive the same surroundings in different ways. Your character's background, personality, and experience will influence what he sees and notices. He may not be able to tell if the décor is neoclassical or Louis XIV, or whether the rug is made of wool or polyester. If these details are important, you could have another character point them out. Or write the scene from a different character's perspective.

Moods

What we see is influenced by how we feel. Filter scenes through the POV character's emotions. This not only lets the reader know how your character feels at that moment but will also set a distinct tone for the scene about to occur in this setting.

Consider the moods created by the following descriptions:

- a basement room lit only by a few small candles, on a stormy night where a gusty wind makes the shutters creak, booming thunder rattles the windows, and flashes of lightning briefly illuminate shadowy corners

- a bustling city street at rush hour, with cars zooming by, belching out gas fumes

- a quiet suburban town at noon, with the aromas of magnolias and freshly cut grass in the air

- a deserted forest at dusk, with limbs smacking the heroine's face, logs making her trip, and a killer in hot pursuit

- a dusty, cluttered attic filled with antiques, stacks of doilies, and bric-a-brac

A particular setting can trigger memories in your character's mind, giving you the opportunity to reveal bits of backstory in a realistic manner. A well-described setting can trigger memories and emotions in your reader as well.

Senses

Use as many of the five senses as you can in each scene, describing things that are seen, touched, tasted, smelled, or heard by the point-of-view character. And show the character's *reaction* to them.

Sight. When a POV character enters a room, describe the appearance gradually. At first, show only what the character notices right away. Let further description unfold as he moves through the room. As you show him doing things there, weave in descriptions that fit the actions.

Let's say you have a woman entering a counselor's office for the first time. Don't describe everything in the room all at once. If she stares at the carpet, give a brief description of the carpet—something specific she notices, and why. If she looks at a picture on the wall, describe the picture and what she thinks of it. When she sits in a chair, describe the chair and its effect on her—does it calm her or make her more agitated?

Make sure you have a good reason behind your choice. Don't pick something randomly. Consider who lives in that room, who owns that furniture. How would that person have decorated the room? What kind of furnishings would that character have bought for that location?

Best-selling author Lena Nelson Dooley says:

Sprinkle snippets of description into the text, slipped in with the conversation beats. Use details that give a feel for the place. Give just what the POV character would notice, especially the things that have an emotional tie for her.

Sometimes a deeper description of the setting can add a colorful or dark layer to the tapestry that serves as the backdrop for your story. But don't make it too long, and always tie bits of it into the POV character's emotions.

Sound. Whatever is *seen* appeals to a reader's mind. Emotions, on the other hand, are more connected with what we *hear*. In conversation, tone of voice is a more reliable indicator of mood and meaning than words. Sounds can make us shudder, jump, relax, or smile. Music creates a powerful ambiance.

Smell. Our sense of smell has the remarkable ability to evoke memories. Describing aromas like bread baking, freshly cut grass, strong perfume, new-car leather, or a wet dog puts your reader into the scene.

Show how the aromas affect the POV character. If she enters a kitchen, dining room, or restaurant, for example, describe the smells that greet her. Do they make her hungry? Nauseated? Homesick?

Weave in the description of the smell at the moment the POV character would experience it. If you walk into a house where a loaf of bread or a batch of cookies has just come out of the oven, you'll smell it the moment you open the door (unless it's a huge house), not when you enter the kitchen.

Touch. Use tactile descriptions when your POV character feels something soft, rough, or warm and when his body feels cold, achy, shivery, or pained.

Taste. The sense of taste is closely related to smell in its ability to evoke emotions. However, taste descriptions must be used sparingly and appropriately—for example, when a character is eating, drinking, brushing his teeth, or gulping salty ocean water. Describe not only the taste but also how that taste affects him.

⚜

Best-selling author Lena Nelson Dooley says:

Every scene should engage two or three of the senses, and all five senses should be used in the story.

Smell. Good or bad, whatever helps the reader become a part of that scene.

Taste. This one is typically used the least, but some tastes should be included in every story.

Touch. Textures, human connections, even painful touching. An emotional scene can be enhanced with an object, such as when the POV character picks up the quilt her departed grandmother made.

Hearing. Not only what the other characters say but also ambient sounds, both inside the room and beyond or outside. Birds singing, crickets chirping, someone gunning a car engine, a mother humming a lullaby.

Sight. Whatever the POV character notices in the context of the scene.

All these senses should evoke some emotional response in the POV character.

Choose specific, vivid details and present them in a way that will capture the reader's attention and allow him to visualize in his mind what you see in yours.

Best-selling author Gail Gaymer Martin says:

Bringing a story to life is more than a sense of place. It's how the place makes the character feel and how it makes the reader feel. Using the senses is important—not only sight and sound, but also taste, touch, and smell. Yet a novel needs even more than that. It's bringing senses to life through the "gut" feeling of the character. His actions show what he is thinking and feeling. It's how he relates to the people and places around him. Consider this paragraph:

> Bill sat in the chair across from his boss's desk. Something was about to happen, but Mr. Undermeyer's face didn't give him a clue.

Now let's bring this to life:

> Bill sank into the chair, his shoulders resisting the cushion. He wanted his boss to think he was alert and interested, but he couldn't fool Mr. Undermeyer. As always, the man's hooded

eyes masked the purpose of the meeting. Bill's gut lurched with each tick of the clock.

Which of these descriptions offers more feeling, more emotion? Have you felt this way? Most of us have, and it helps readers know they aren't alone when feeling uncertain or facing trouble.

⇌⊹⊱⊰⊹⇌

Show the character's *reaction* or *response* to the setting. What happens when she sits in the chaise lounge, looks out the dirty window, or sees her hometown for the first time in twenty years? What emotions do dark, ominous clouds invoke that puffy white clouds don't?

Get the Details Right

Descriptions add authenticity. If you're writing a story that takes place in a location you aren't familiar with, do your research. If at all possible, visit the place (or a similar one) and record what you see, hear, smell, taste, and feel. Then write vivid descriptions that set the tone for your scenes and make your readers feel as if they are really there.

Chapter 17

EDITING FICTION—DIALOGUE

Dialogue is what your characters say out loud. It is always placed inside quotation marks.

Fictional dialogue should simulate speech, but it should not be written the way people actually talk. In real life, people leave out words, compress phrases into single words, repeat favorite phrases, and use clichés. They pause to think about what they're saying and consequently mumble sounds like *um* and *er* as well as insert meaningless words like *well, like, so,* and *you know.*

Real speech is impromptu, and people often talk when they have nothing important to say. But fictional characters must have a reason to speak. Every line of dialogue should fulfill one or more of the following purposes:

- advance the plot

- reveal character

- disclose motivation

- establish tone or mood

If a line of dialogue doesn't fill at least one of these criteria, delete it.

Common Dialogue Mistakes

Here are some of the most common mistakes new writers make with dialogue.

Dialect

"Dat feller sed ah shoulda jes' kep' runnin' ta kitch ep wit' da rist o' 'em." How long did it take you to figure out that line of dialogue?

And can you imagine how long it will take to run spell-check on a manuscript full of dialect?

If it's important to show a character's accent, use these techniques:

- narrative ("She spoke with a delightful Georgia drawl.")
- word choice and speech patterns ("Why, you sweet little peach blossom, I do declare you get prettier every time I set my eyes on you" or "That there bonnie lass is carrying a wee bairn in her belly, I'd stake my pot of gold on it.")

You heard accents in your head when you read those, didn't you?

Minor dialect may be used sparingly—for example, dropping g's or alternate spellings that are instantly distinguishable. ("Ya fixin' to eat yer vittles?") But overuse of this can become irritating to readers and is unnecessary if the word choice and narrative make the accent clear.

Awkward Speech

Use words and phrases consistent with the character's age, background, and occupation. Most young children use simple words. A modern American teenager would probably call her father "Dad" and would use contractions and slang.

Unless you're writing a period piece, eliminate terms that will date your manuscript—contemporary slang or references to celebrities who may no longer be popular when your book is read.

Name Calling

Don't have your characters use each other's names as an easy way to identify who's speaking to whom. In real life, people rarely use each other's names in conversation.

Listen to some actual conversations, keeping track of how often people say the other person's name—and in what circumstances. Typically, we only do this is when we're trying to get someone's attention, show a high level of respect, or make a specific point. For example:

"George Anthony Michaels, you stop that this instant."

"Yes, Mr. Peterson, whatever you say."

"Charlie, are you listening to me?"

"Mark! I'm over here!"

Fancy Words

Don't use words that your target audience may be unfamiliar with, unless the meaning is immediately obvious from the context.

Best-selling author Gail Gaymer Martin says:

Avoid "million dollar" words. If readers don't know a word, they stop and look it up or ponder what it means. Although you might like using a $$$ word, you put the reader at a disadvantage. Keep the vocabulary in the POV character's tone and verbal style, making sure the words fit your character's education, experience, and career. Use language that most people can pronounce and understand.

Incorrect Paragraphing

The actions and speech of a character should be in the same paragraph. Start a new paragraph to designate a change in speaker. Here's an example:

The flight attendant paused in the aisle. "Something to drink for you?"

"Ginger ale?" Mary's tummy wasn't roiling yet, but the pilot had announced turbulence ahead.

The young woman in the crisp navy-blue uniform passed a plastic cup to Mary over the sleeping passenger in the aisle seat. As Mary took it, the plane bounced, spilling the bubbly drink all over the businessman's expensive-looking suit. He sat up with a jolt.

"I'm so sorry," Mary and the flight attendant said at the same time.

All Characters Sounding Alike

Your characters shouldn't all sound like you. Each one should have a unique voice, including speech patterns and word choices.

Long, Uninterrupted Speeches

Don't let one character talk too long. If you must show someone giving a speech (a pastor's sermon, for example), hit only the highlights, and intersperse the monologue with narrative. Wherever possible, insert interruptions, such as other characters speaking or the POV character's thoughts, actions, and observations.

Improper Order

You want to include action, dialogue, and the POV character's internal thoughts in your scenes. But the order in which you show those things is crucial.

Best-selling author Angela Hunt says:

When you wish to show emotion, action, and dialogue together, they should be written in that order: feeling, then action, then speech. You can delete the feeling if it is evident in the action. Here's an example:

Original: "Get out of my office!" He slammed the desk. Anger rose inside him.

Better: He slammed the desk. "Get out of my office!"

The only exception is if the speech logically comes before the feeling or action.

Example: "I remember this picture." She touched the faded photograph as nostalgia swept over her.

Subtext

People don't always say what they mean. Your characters shouldn't either.

Best-selling author Brandilyn Collins says:

The biggest dialogue problem I see from many novelists is that the dialogue is "on the nose"—that is, every character says exactly what he's thinking. People don't talk like that. Lots of times, their words are on one level, and the meaning lies underneath. This is called subtext.

Of course, some dialogue should be WYSIWYG (what you see is what you get). The trick is knowing when to subtext.

Real people have two main reasons for not saying what they mean: (1) They don't want to admit what they're really thinking, or (2) They don't need to say what they're thinking because the other person already knows it.

As you talk to people and overhear conversations, or while you're reading or watching TV or a movie, be alert for subtext in dialogue. You'll notice that bits of meaning are found in four categories of description surrounding the spoken words: Thought, Inflection, Movement, and Expression (TIME).

Thought. This is the easiest technique to employ, so it's also easy to overuse. Don't simply move all meaning from spoken word to narrative thought. This will negate the need for other kinds of description and will deaden your scene, telling your story rather than showing it.

Inflection. One or two well-chosen words can convey a magnitude of meaning.

Movement. A slouch, a jiggling foot, a flick of the hand—all convey messages.

Expression. Facial expression can tell the reader far more than words.[19]

❈❈❈❈❈

Speaker Attributions

It's important to let readers know who's speaking each line of dialogue. There are two ways to do this.

Dialogue Tags

Dialogue tags (such as "he said" and "she asked") tell readers who is speaking. Since the word *said* is virtually invisible to the reader, it can be used repeatedly throughout a manuscript. Feel free to occasionally use an unobtrusive synonym for *said* (*asked, replied, answered*). However, don't resort to flowery synonyms for *said* (*retorted, insinuated, interjected, protested, uttered, crowed, pleaded, pointed out*).

Also avoid using adverbs to describe how something is said. For example, don't write, "she replied mournfully" or "he said enthusiastically."

Make it obvious from the dialogue, actions, body language, and the POV character's thoughts how something is said, rather than telling the reader in the dialogue tag. If a reader can tell that the words were cried, hollered, or whispered (as should be the case most of the time), the descriptive attribution becomes redundant.

---

[19] Excerpted from *Getting into Character: Seven Secrets a Novelist Can Learn from Actors.* For more about this book, see http://brandilyncollins.com/books/nonfiction/getting_into_character/.

Best-selling author Gail Gaymer Martin says:

Don't use tag words other than *said* and *asked*.

"How have you been?" she queried.

Obviously she's querying by the nature of the sentence.

Use a comma to connect the attributive tag to the dialogue. Example:

"This is how attribution should be written," Joan told the class.

Beware of impossible attributions, such as a line of dialogue followed by a comma and "he choked" or "she giggled" or some other action that cannot be performed while speaking.

You can combine a dialogue tag with an action, facial expression, tone of voice, body language, or internal thought—as long as the point-of-view character is in a position to see or hear or think it. For example:

"Where are you going?" he asked, his voice trembling.

"I don't know," she replied as she tucked her child into the car seat.

Best-selling author Gail Gaymer Martin says:

Cutting tags allows tension to be more prominent. For example, you could write:

"Stop it," she said, "you're hurting me."

If you drop the *she said*, you have:

"Stop it. You're hurting me."

The tighter line helps to dramatize the tension.

As long as the speaker is clear, you can present dialogue without any beats. But a few beats can add reality to the scene and illuminate a character. They also provide breathing space, giving the reader a break from the constant rifle shot of dialogue.

⫷⊱⊰⊹⊱⊰⫸

Too many dialogue tags can come across as lazy or contrived writing. The best way to get rid of some of those pesky tags is to replace them with narrative beats.

Narrative Beats

You can show action in the same paragraph as the dialogue when the person speaking performs the action. Example:

Mary grinned. "I can't wait to tell John the latest gossip."

Narrative beats are often more effective than speaker attributions because they can convey action, characterization, setting, and background while identifying the speaker. Example:

Tim tightened the last screw on the ship model. "I can't believe this is finally done."

A narrative beat can also reveal a character's emotion. Instead of writing, "he said angrily," show the character's body stiffening, his face turning red, his voice dropping to a whisper, or his fists clenching.

If the internal emotion differs from what the words imply, show something in the narrative that clues the reader in to the real emotion behind the words. Example:

John spat on the ground. "I can't wait to see her again."

Narrative beats should be separated from dialogue by a period, not a comma, since they are complete sentences. Here's an example of the proper formatting:

> Madeleine looked up from her knitting when her husband walked in the door. "Did you go to the store today?"
>
> "No." Harry took off his windbreaker. "Why do you ask?"
>
> "I mentioned this morning that we're out of milk and bread." She sighed, wondering what she was going to do with this forgetful man.

In addition to getting rid of the dialogue tags, narrative beats help the reader envision what's happening in the scene.

Beats also provide a pause in the dialogue or action. The longer the narrative, the longer the pause. In general, the amount of time it takes to read the narrative should be approximately equivalent to the time that lapses in the scene.

❦

Best-selling author Deborah Raney says:

Avoid most speaker attributions other than *said*. But don't be too quick to kill *all* attributions. It's better to have too many "he said/she saids" than for your reader to be confused about who is speaking. And sometimes those attributions add an important element of rhythm and timing to your dialogue. If in doubt, read the line aloud to see if it sounds better with or without the attribution.

❦

Tags and Beats

By combining both methods, you won't have the same sentence structure occur so often that it's noticeable to the reader.

Tags or Beats

Using both a narrative beat and speaker attribution in the same paragraph is redundant and should be avoided.

> Example: Sam clenched his fists. "You can't fire me," he said. (The "he said" is unnecessary.)

Best-selling author Lena Nelson Dooley says:

Conversation beats can be actions, internal thoughts, or what the POV character sees.

Not every line of dialogue needs a conversation tag or beat, especially in a fast-moving story like a suspense novel. If it's obvious who's speaking, a tag or beat is superfluous and slows the pace. But even with suspense, the reader needs time to breathe.

Many of my books don't have a single conversation tag in them. They take up word count without adding anything to the story. I want every word to count.

See how much deeper you can pull the reader into the emotions or action of your story by replacing as many conversation tags with beats as possible. And eliminate both tags and beats when you can without making your reader go back and reread to figure out who said what.

I never have more than three or four bits of dialogue without some kind of beat or tag.

Act It Out

Read the dialogue in your manuscript out loud, one character at a time. Start with your main character. Read every scene that's in his perspective, skipping any scenes that are out of his POV. Then do the same for everyone else in your story.

Listen for places where the dialogue sounds forced, stilted, unrealistic, or contrary to that character's personality and background. This will give you a good feel for each distinct voice, and you'll be able to tell when something is off. It will also clue you in to areas where a character is in a scene but silent for long periods of time.

Are there any long gaps where someone stands around in a scene but doesn't speak? Does he say or do anything that would require knowledge of scenes in which he was not present?

Then have someone else read each character's dialogue while you listen.

Picture an actor playing your character and saying those lines of dialogue.

Also, act out the motions mentioned in the text—again, one character at a time. Consider having one or more friends act out the other characters' motions. Watch for places where an individual stands when he is already standing, sits when he is already sitting, stops being involved in a scene without actually leaving the area, or fails to react appropriately. Look for places where a character or object suddenly appears or disappears in a scene.

Chapter 18

FINE-TUNE EDIT

Before you send your manuscript to an agent, publishing house, subsidy publisher, or printer, give it a final polish. This will greatly increase your ability to attract the attention of a traditional publisher. If you self-publish, this last step will make you and your work look professional.

Thorough Proofread

Make sure the punctuation, usage, grammar, and spelling (what I call PUGS) are correct. One comma in the wrong place can change the meaning of a sentence. And mechanical errors will make you look like an amateur to readers and publishers.

Review the nuts and bolts of punctuation and grammar by consulting *The Chicago Manual of Style,* the industry-standard reference for traditional book publishers in the US. Be sure to use the most recent edition.

If you can't get a copy of *The Chicago Manual of Style,* can't find what you're looking for in it, or can't understand it when you do, you may wish to purchase the first book in this series, *Proofreading Secrets of Best-Selling Authors.* It contains guidelines based on CMOS, but the material is organized in a more user-friendly fashion and written in easier-to-understand terms.

Use a spell-checker to catch typos your eyes don't pick up on, but don't expect it to find every misspelled or misused word in your manuscript. Look up everything you're not 100 percent sure of in the most recent edition of *Merriam-Webster's Collegiate Dictionary,* the industry standard for traditional book publishers in the US. (Consult Merriam-Webster.com for spelling of modern terms.) Study the definition to make sure the word is what you meant to use and you have the correct spelling for that form of speech. Look up all hyphenated words and compound words.

Visual Overview

Look at each page without reading the words, analyzing only how it looks visually. Does any page have so much text that the thought of reading it makes your head hurt?

Best-selling author Deborah Raney says:

Print out your manuscript and look over each page with an eye to the graphic, visual look of it. Plenty of white space makes a book more appealing and reader-friendly. Are there paragraphs or series of paragraphs on a page that are too long, making for an intimidating block of type? If so, break the scene into shorter paragraphs or add a bit of dialogue to incorporate some white space on the page. Remember, a lack of dialogue for several pages may mean you are *telling* rather than *showing*—a good way to risk losing your reader.

If you're preparing a nonfiction manuscript to be printed (as opposed to formatting an e-book), do a manual search for hyperlinks. They'll usually show up in a different-colored font, probably underlined. If you find any, right-click on it and select Remove Hyperlink.

Formatting Review

When submitting to agents or book publishers, follow their guidelines. In the absence of instructions to the contrary, follow the standard formatting for traditional publishing houses given below.

Complete Manuscript File

All margins should be one inch.

In Settings, uncheck Widow and Orphan Control. (If you don't know how to accomplish this, do an internet search for the program you use.)

Title Page

One-third of the way down the first page, type the title of your book in ALL CAPS. If you have a subtitle, type that in Initial Caps on the next line. (See *Proofreading Secrets of Best-Selling Authors* for guidelines on which words to capitalize in a title.) Two lines down from that, type your name (or your pen name, if you wish to use one). This should all be centered, with no left indent.

At the bottom of the page, left aligned, type your real name. On the next line, type your mailing address; on the third line, your city, state, and zip code. On the fourth line, type your phone number with area code. On the subsequent line(s), type your email address and/or website URL.

Do not add a copyright line. Your work is automatically copyright protected, so putting the © symbol on your work brands you as an amateur. Reputable agents and publishers wouldn't dream of ripping off an author's work, so it's a bit insulting to suggest that you fear this.

Do not put a page number on the title page.

Header

At the top of every page except the Title Page, insert a header using the header feature. Flush left, type your last name, slash, and book title. If your book title is long, use a few key words from it. Put a running page number in the upper-right corner.

Text

To ensure that all of your text is formatted correctly, select the entire manuscript. Then follow these steps.

1. In the Font section, use these settings:
    *   Times New Roman
    *   12 point
    *   automatic/black

2. In the Paragraph section, use these settings:
    *   Alignment: Left
    *   First-line indent: .5 inch
    *   Spacing before and after: 0 pts.
    *   Line spacing: double

Then go through your manuscript, center the chapter titles, and take out the automatic left indent on all centered lines.

Use the Find and Replace feature to fix the following issues:

1. Remove extra spaces between sentences.
    a. Type two spaces in the Find box.
    b. Type one space in the Replace box.
    c. Click Replace All until the number gets to zero.

2. Remove spaces at the beginnings of paragraphs.
    a. Type ^p and a space in the Find box.
    b. Type ^p in the Replace box.
    c. Click Replace All until the number gets to zero.

3. Remove spaces at the ends of paragraphs.
    a. Type a space and ^p in the Find box.
    b. Type ^p in the Replace box.
    c. Click Replace All until the number gets to zero.

4. Remove spaces before and after em dashes.
    a. Type a space and ^+ in the Find box.
    b. Type ^+ (without the space) in the Replace box.
    c. Click Replace All until the number gets to zero.
    d. Type ^+ and a space in the Find box.

e. Type ^+ (without the space) in the Replace box.

f. Click Replace All until the number gets to zero.

5. Remove spaces before and after en dashes.

a. Type a space and ^= in the Find box.

b. Type ^= (without the space) in the Replace box.

c. Click Replace All until the number gets to zero.

d. Type ^= and a space in the Find box.

e. Type ^= (without the space) in the Replace box.

f. Click Replace All until the number gets to zero.

6. Make all apostrophes and quotation marks "smart" (curly).

a. Set your computer options for "smart quotes." (If you type a quotation mark or apostrophe and it comes out curly, your options are set correctly.)

b. Type a quotation mark in the Find box.

c. Type a quotation mark in the Replace box.

d. Click Replace All.

e. Type an apostrophe in the Find box.

f. Type an apostrophe in the Replace box.

g. Click Replace All.

Then do a search for apostrophes curled the wrong way.

a. Type a space and an apostrophe in the Find box.

b. Since Word assumes that an apostrophe at the beginning of a word is a single quotation mark, it will have curled it that way. If you meant it to be an apostrophe (e.g., in the word 'tis), type another apostrophe to the right of the one in the text. That will curl the right way. Then delete the one that's curled the wrong way (e.g., 'tis).

Chapters

Start each chapter on a new page using Insert/Page break. Do not insert a bunch of blank lines to get to the next page.

About one-third of the way down the page, centered, type CHAPTER 1 (2, 3, etc.) or CHAPTER ONE (TWO, THREE, etc.). On the next line, type the chapter title (if you have one), centered, with initial caps ("Initial Caps for Chapter Titles"). Insert one or two blank lines before starting the text. (Make sure you're consistent throughout the manuscript with how many blank lines you have above the chapter number and between the chapter number/title and the text.)

Paragraphs

Indent the first line of every paragraph, including the first one in a chapter or section, one-half inch using automatic first-line indentation. Do not use multiple spaces or tabs. Don't add blank lines between paragraphs. Take out any automatic paragraph spacing your word-processing program may add.

Quotations that are more than four lines long should be block-indented. You may also block-indent quotations you want to highlight. These should be left aligned, like the rest of the text, with an extra half inch added to the left margin only.

Words

Do not use ALL CAPS or **bold** for emphasis. If you must emphasize something, italicize it. But don't overdo that.

Underlining of text that is to be *italicized* when the book goes to print used to be the standard. But since typesetting is now computerized, publishers want italicized text to be italicized in the author's manuscript.

Chapter 19

PROFESSIONAL EDIT

No matter how well you've self-edited your manuscript, a good freelance editor will find ways to polish it further, making it more powerful, clear, and effective, and therefore more attractive to agents, publishers, and readers.

Yes, a professional edit will cost you money. But how much time and effort have you put into your writing already? If you wanted to join the church choir, a passion to sing and the ability to carry a tune may be all you need. But if you wanted to embark on a singing career, wouldn't you hire a music coach? If you're hoping that people, other than your friends and family, will want to read what you've written—and pay for it—you'll need to invest financially in your manuscript and your possible future career.

Best-selling author Kathleen Y'Barbo says:

Why would an author need a professional edit? Simple. We carry worlds of people and situations in our heads when we're writing, and we hope all of that has translated to the page. But has it? Only a professional edit will answer that question. An editor will ensure not only that everything you wanted to say is there but that you said it in a clear, concise, correct manner. There's no substitute for a professional edit!

When to Start Looking

If you're just beginning to think about writing for publication, you don't need an editor. Learn writing skills first. While a freelance editor can be a great writing teacher, you may be able to get what you need at this stage from reading books on writing, taking classes, or attending a writers' conference and talking with other authors.

If you've written a few short pieces or a few chapters of a book, a critique partner or group would be invaluable. If you haven't been able to find a good critique group or partner, a freelance editor can help you polish your manuscript, and you'll learn writing techniques along the way.

If you think your manuscript is ready to submit to an agent or publisher, hiring a freelance editor before submitting will optimize your chances of acceptance.

If you've self-edited to the point where you don't want to look at your manuscript anymore, a freelance editor can provide fresh insights that will reignite your passion.

If you're planning to self-publish, you should definitely hire an editor. You don't want to publish your book and discover too late that it contains mistakes.

If you think your manuscript is perfect and wonderful and straight from God's lips to your fingertips, and all you want is someone to tell you so, don't bother hiring an editor. Let friends and family give you the encouragement and raves you desire. An editor's job is to show you how your manuscript can be improved and what errors need to be corrected.

❦

Best-selling author Eva Marie Everson says:

As president of Word Weavers International, I'm often asked, "Why should I have my work professionally edited?" I often find that these folks have had their work "looked at" by an English teacher or "a friend who reads a lot" and they believe this should be sufficient. No.

Even taking your work to a critique group is not 100 percent because the work has been looked at piecemeal. I tell these authors that a professional edit will bring them and their work a step above the rest. It says to an acquisitions editor or agent that *they* are professionals as well because they are looking at the work as more than just inspired words on paper. Publishing is a professional industry. Treat it thusly.

Where to Find an Editor

You could do an internet search for freelance editors. But that will result in a deluge of links to people who claim to be professional freelance editors. How can you know which ones are good ... or even legitimate?

If you know writers who've worked with editors, you could ask them for referrals.

If you attend writers' conferences, you will likely meet freelance editors, and they may have flyers on a freebie table you could pick up. If you make a personal connection at a conference, conduct due diligence to make sure the editor has the skills you need.

If you think you might like to have me edit your manuscript, email me for a quote at Kathy@KathyIde.com. If you'd like to consider other options, check out the Christian Editor Connection. CEC has a database of established, professional editors who have been extensively screened and tested. If you go to ChristianEditor.com and fill out the form to Request an Editor, you will be personally matched with editors who fit your parameters and requirements: genre, type of editing, and any specific requests you make. Those editors who are interested and available will email you directly. You may then contact those editors, check out their websites, and communicate with them to determine which is the best choice for you.

This is, in my opinion, the best way to find the right editor.

Cost

Some editors charge by the hour, others by the page or word. Some charge a percentage of the estimated total up front, with another percentage midway through the project and a final payment at the end. Others require payment in full up front.

Many writers prefer a cost per page or word, believing that will provide a solid amount they can plan on for their full edit. But make sure you understand what's included in that total. Often the first edit of a manuscript is just the beginning. The editor will make suggestions you'll need to implement, after which you'll probably need a second pass.

Also, keep in mind that an editor who charges by the page or word knows how much she wants to make per hour, and she has calculated her rate based on a worst-case scenario. If your manuscript is more polished than average, you might be paying the same amount as someone who has submitted a rough draft without even bothering to run spell-check.

If you choose an editor who charges by the hour, the more polished your manuscript is when you send it in, the less time it will take to edit—which will save you money in the long run. And if you pick up on recurring corrections and suggestions in the initial edit and implement what you learned in subsequent chapters before sending them, you'll save more money.

The total cost for an edit of your manuscript may seem like a hefty expenditure of cash. But I like to think of working with a professional freelance editor as taking an in-depth writing course, with your manuscript as the lesson plan. How much would you pay for a personal writing tutor?

Best-selling author Lori Freeland says:

No matter how much we know, how great our skill set, or how many books we've written, it's nearly impossible to see our own errors. Because we created the story, our brains automatically fill in the gaps and fix the issues. I edit and teach writing classes for a living, but I still need someone to check my work. Fresh eyes from a knowledgeable source are essential for a solid final draft. You've done a lot of the hard work—take it through to the end. Invest in a good editor to make your manuscript the best it can be.

Choosing the Right One

You've narrowed down your search to a few editors who all seem qualified. How can you determine which is the right one for you?

Visit their websites to get a feel for the editors' personalities, background, and experience. Get a quote on their services and rates. Communicate via phone or email. Some editors prefer connecting by phone, others by email. If you have a strong preference, choose an editor who has the same preference.

You could start with a short piece, the first few chapters of your book, or a proposal. You'll learn a lot from that initial edit that you can apply to everything you write. Some editors offer free sample edits of one or two pages. However, editors who have a lot of paid projects on their calendars may charge a small fee to do a sample edit for a potential client.

While the saying "You get what you pay for" is true, if you're a new writer, a new editor may work well for you. If you're self-publishing for family and friends, a beginning editor is probably okay. If you're an intermediate writer, you should choose at least an intermediate-level editor. If you want the most for your money, be willing to hire the best editor you can afford.

Look for an editor who specializes in your type of writing and your genre. Don't ask an editor who works with nonfiction to edit your novel. If you write sci-fi/fantasy or poetry, find an editor who knows the unique requirements and techniques for that type of writing.

You could ask a potential editor if she's published anything of her own. But writing and editing are very different skills. Writing is right-brained—creative. Editing is left-brained—analytical. People who are really good at one skill may not be particularly adept at the other. In addition, writing for publication requires a significant investment of time. An editor who has chosen to focus on editing rather than writing her own books may be an excellent choice.

Personality compatibility can be a valuable commodity in the author-editor relationship. If you feel comfortable with your editor as a person, you may be less hesitant to ask questions about why she made certain comments. On the other hand, if you see your editor as a friend, you might chafe at some of the seemingly harsh comments she might make from time to time.

If you know that you work better with people who are the same gender as you, that might be a consideration. However, don't discount the potential benefits of getting a different perspective from someone of the opposite sex. This is especially important if you have characters in your novel that aren't the same gender as you.

You might want to consider choosing an editor who represents your target audience—unless you're writing books for children or snarky teenagers.

If you find an editor who is passionate about your writing and your project, that might make the collaboration a bit more fun.

Best-selling author Cindy Woodsmall says:

An editor is similar to available water in a kitchen. When buying or building a home, we take every aspect of a kitchen into consideration except running water, but without it, very little else is useful enough to matter.

What to Expect

When you hire a professional freelance editor, here's what you can expect:

- Professionalism—but not perfection. Nobody's perfect ... not even editors.

- Confidentiality. If editors stole their clients' work, they wouldn't stay in business very long. Besides, editors who wish to write books already have their own ideas for what to write about.

- Honesty. An objective analysis of the manuscript's strengths and weakness—no false hopes or random criticism.

- Encouragement. Pointing out what's good and working in addition to what needs improvement.

- Communication. But don't expect your editor to respond to every email within an hour. Editors have lives too. If your editor has a Coming Events page on her website, a Facebook page, and/or a newsletter, you might want to check those if you haven't heard from her in a few days.

- Promptness. Returning your edit within the promised turnaround time, if at all possible. But keep in mind, life happens. Even to editors. If you don't get your manuscript back when you were expecting it, contact the editor and ask if things are still on schedule or if life events may have extended the lead time a bit.

Contracts

Some editors use contracts or agreements; others do not. If you pay a percentage up front, another percentage midway through, and a final payment at the end, the editor will likely have a contract that specifies what work will be done in each phase and what happens if work is done and not paid for.

If you pay for a certain number of hours in advance, a contract may not be necessary. The editor will work the amount of time you paid for, and if you're not pleased with the results, you don't have to pay for additional hours.

If you hire someone to rewrite, ghostwrite, collaborate, or coauthor with you, there should be a contract that specifies details like rights, royalties, and bylines.

If your editor doesn't offer a contract, but you'd feel more comfortable having one, feel free to ask.

Editorial Services

Some editors, especially very right-brained ones, excel at providing an overall critique or content edit. Others, especially strongly left-brained ones, tend to be more skilled at line-by-line copyediting, which typically includes an organizational edit and the scissors edit described in this book. Some editors are able to do both kinds of editing simultaneously.

If you're concerned about the overall content of your manuscript, you may want a content edit (aka critique or developmental edit). When you're reasonably satisfied with your content, you could move on to a copyedit. If you want to save time and/or money, you may wish to find an editor who can do both at the same time.

After you go through the editing process, before sending your manuscript (or anything else) to an agent or acquisitions editor or publisher/printer, be sure to get a thorough proofread—preferably from a professional.

Levels of Editing

There are several types of editorial services, and different editors may have slightly different definitions of the terms. You can find some basic terms and definitions on the Christian Editor Connection website (www.ChristianEditor.com/types-of-editing), but be sure to communicate with your editor what you're looking for as well as what the editor believes your manuscript needs.

Prepare Yourself

If you go through the steps in this book before hiring a professional editor, you will likely pay far less than someone who sends in a rough draft. If you study *Proofreading Secrets of Best-Selling Authors,* and the industry-standard reference books it's based on, your cost for a professional proofread will be far less than for someone who doesn't.

Even if you've studied self-editing and proofreading, and worked hard on your manuscript, you may be surprised at how many marks the editor will make on your manuscript. So while you're waiting to receive the edited version, adjust your expectations.

If you do freak out when you see all those changes, set the manuscript aside for a while. Vent to a friend. Kick a cabinet or two—preferably in steel-toed shoes. Remind yourself that your editor wants to help you improve your manuscript—that's what you paid her for. After you've calmed down, look at the manuscript one change at a time.

Seeing a lot of markings on your manuscript doesn't necessarily mean there's so much wrong with it you should give up trying to write. The editor may just see several ways that you could make the manuscript even better than it already is.

Your edit will likely include two types of changes: corrections and suggestions. The corrections—typos, misspelled words, grammar and punctuation errors—should definitely be made. The suggestions are the editors' opinions, based on her years in the publishing industry. Seriously consider them. After all, if you took your baby to a doctor and he said, "Here's what's wrong with your child and what you can do to make him healthier," you'd do it, right? Unless you had a really good reason not to, like a second opinion from another professional.

If you're not sure why the editor made a change, ask for clarification.

But remember, this is your book and your name will be on the cover. So make the changes you believe work best for you and for your book.

For more tips on getting a professional edit, check out *Finding and Working with an Editor: Everything You Need to Know for a (Nearly) Pain-Free Edit* by best-selling author Karen Ball and Erin Taylor Young.

Discounts on My Services

In my *Proofreading Secrets of Best-Selling Authors,* I offered anyone who purchased that book a $5/hour discount on my editing services. I figured people who had my book would be able to proofread their manuscripts according to the guidelines presented there, which would make my job easier.

I'm making that same offer to those who purchase *Editing Secrets of Best-Selling Authors.* If you implement the techniques described in this book, your manuscript will be more polished, which will enable me to go deeper in helping you take it to the next level.

If you purchase both books, I will combine the discounts and give you $10/hour off my standard rate. If you're interested in finding out more, email me at Kathy@KathyIde.com.

Chapter 20

WHEN TO STOP EDITING

Writers can become so focused on perfecting their work that they can't quit. As a result, they never complete a book manuscript and get it published because it's never quite ready. Or they edit the life out of their work.

Best-selling author Kathleen Y'Barbo says:

Some authors don't know when to stop working on their completed manuscript. I am not suggesting that you turn out a substandard product, but at some point, you have to let it go. Guess what? It's never going to be perfect. Ask any published author if she wouldn't jump at the chance to tweak her books that are already in print. And these novels have been through multiple edits. So perhaps your problem isn't perfectionism. Maybe your real issue is fear. Fear of rejection. Or maybe fear of success. If so, ask yourself, *What am I afraid of? What's the opposition that's keeping me from moving forward?*

Over-editing steals your energy and creativity.

How to Avoid Over-Editing

If you're a perfectionist, how do you keep from constantly editing?

Set a Deadline

Give yourself a penalty if you don't meet a deadline, even if it's self-imposed. No chocolate the next day. No TV in the evening. Alternatively, reward yourself for meeting the deadline.

Best-selling author Deborah Raney says:

I turn in almost every manuscript at five p.m. on the day it's due. A few years ago, it was 5:05 when I finally emailed my first draft to my editor, along with an apology for being a few minutes late. "Actually," he replied, "I'm working on the West Coast this week. You're two hours early!"

My instant response: "Then I want it back!"

I don't know any seasoned author who ever feels her manuscript is ready to turn in when the deadline rolls around. There are always a few more tweaks we'd like to make. But eventually, we must loosen our grip on our precious words and press Send.

List Common Problems

Working on a list of specific problem areas will help you stay focused. Once you fix an area of weakness, let it go and move on to the next one.

Best-selling author Gail Gaymer Martin says:

I write without editing until I'm done for the day. When I return to the novel, I go back to what I've written and reread, making a few changes or highlighting a section I'm not sure about or one that needs some research. Then I continue to write, adding more to the story. When I stop, I go back and fix the things I highlighted earlier that need work, or I wait and edit the next day. But each day I only edit what I wrote the day before. Once I have five or six chapters written, I edit again, and then move forward with the novel. I always leave a note to myself where I will start when I finish writing for the day or if I'm taking a break.

Walk Away

Give yourself a break from the book. Put it aside for a few days and allow yourself to disengage from it. When you go back, you can look at it with fresh eyes. What seemed amazing when you wrote it might not work so well after all. What felt off earlier might seem perfect now.

Best-selling author Mona Hodgson says:

I had to learn to let go of perfectionism in order to embrace productivity. I love to edit! Polishing my story to make it shine is like a drug to me. The more I do, the more I want to do. If I embrace my perfectionism tendencies, I let go of productivity. Instead, I pull in a deep breath and determine when enough is enough, then happily move on to write something else I'll get to edit!

Chapter 21

TAKE THIS JOB AND LOVE IT

The more you edit your manuscript, the more you'll realize that writing it was the easy part! But as you read your revised work, I am confident you will see how much better it is—that it reads more smoothly, communicates more clearly, and has more power to touch readers' hearts and maybe even change their lives.

And who knows? At some point, you might discover that you enjoy editing more than writing. If that turns out to be the case, check out Christian Editor Network. Its four divisions are designed to equip, empower, and encourage aspiring and established editors in the Christian market.

- The Christian PEN: Proofreaders and Editors Network provides an email forum, monthly e-newsletters, and special discounts.
- The PEN Institute offers a wide range of online educational opportunities for editors at all stages.
- PENCON is an annual conference for freelance and in-house editors.
- Christian Editor Connection matches authors, publishers, and agents with established professional editorial freelancers based on their specific needs.

Whether you're looking to start a freelance editing business, make an existing one more successful, find encouragement through networking, or connect with potential new clients, Christian Editor Network can help. Visit christianeditornetwork.com.

Enjoy the Journey

I hope you find the tips in this book beneficial as you edit your own writing, help your critique partners with their manuscripts, or work as a freelance editor. Polishing rough drafts to make them shine requires a significant amount of time, effort, focus, and development of skills that are different from those needed to write a first draft. The end result will be well worth the investment. But don't forget to have fun along the way. You are creating something unique and special. Enjoy the journey.

Appendix A

RECOMMENDED RESOURCES
Compiled by Kathy Ide

GENERAL

Bird by Bird by Anne Lamott
On Writing by Stephen King
On Writing Well by William Zinsser
Techniques of the Selling Writer by Dwight Swain

NONFICTION TECHNIQUES

How to Get Your Book Published by Robert W. Bly
How to Publish Your Articles by Shirley Kawa-Jump
Writing Creative Nonfiction, edited by Carolyn Forche
Writing Successful Self-Help & How-to Books by Jean Marie Stine

MEMOIR

Inventing the Truth: The Art and Craft of Memoir (a compilation from multiple authors)
Writing & Selling Your Memoir by Paula Balzer

FICTION TECHNIQUES

The Art & Craft of Novel Writing by Oakley Hall
Creating Characters by Dwight Swain
Creating Fiction, a compilation edited by Julie Checkoway
The Fire in Fiction by Donald Maas
Getting into Character: Seven Secrets a Novelist Can Learn from Actors by Brandilyn Collins
Plot and Structure by James Scott Bell

Practical Tips for Writing Popular Fiction by Robyn Carr
Self-editing for Fiction Writers by Renni Browne and Dave King
Story by Robert McKee
Writing the Blockbuster Novel by Albert Zuckerman
Writing the Breakout Novel by Donald Maas

SPECIALIZING

The Art & Craft of Playwriting by Jeffrey Hatcher
Christian Drama Publishing by Kathy Ide
How to Write Science Fiction and Fantasy by Orson Scott Card
Writing for Children & Teenagers by Lee Wyndham
Writing Mysteries, a compilation edited by Sue Grafton
That's Not the Way It Works: A No-Nonsense Guide to the Craft and Business of Screenwriting by Bob Saenz

REFERENCE BOOKS

The Associated Press Stylebook (for articles)
The Chicago Manual of Style (for book manuscripts)
The Christian Writer's Manual of Style (for specifically Christian issues)
Merriam-Webster's Collegiate Dictionary (for book manuscripts)
Webster's New World College Dictionary (for articles)
Proofreading Secrets of Best-Selling Authors by Kathy Ide (for books and articles)

Also check out your favorite writers' websites. Many multi-published authors, including the ones quoted in this book, have tips for writers on their sites or blogs. Many literary agents offer online tips as well.

APPENDIX B

CONTRIBUTING AUTHOR BIOS

Editing tips in this book were graciously provided by the following best-selling authors (listed in alphabetical order by last name).

James Scott Bell (jamesscottbell.com) is the author of *Plot & Structure* and *Revision & Self-Editing* as well as thriller novels. Jim attended the University of California–Santa Barbara, where he studied writing with Raymond Carver. He graduated with honors from the University of Southern California law school and has written more than three hundred articles and several books for the legal profession. He has taught novel writing at Pepperdine University and numerous conferences in the United States, Canada, and Great Britain.

Brandilyn Collins (brandilyncollins.com) has written almost thirty books. Most are in her Seatbelt Suspense® novel line; others are in the contemporary genre. Her novels have won several awards, including the ACFW Carol (three times), Inspirational Readers' Choice, Romantic Times Reviewers' Choice, the Inspy, and Christian Retailers' Best Award (twice).

Lena Nelson Dooley (lenanelsondooley.com) has more than 900,000 copies of her fifty-plus books in print. She is a frequent speaker at women's groups, writers' groups, and regional and national conferences. Her books have appeared on the CBA, *Publishers Weekly,* and ECPA best-seller lists, as well as Amazon best-seller lists. They have received numerous awards, including the Will Rogers Medallion, Selah, NTRWA Carolyn Reader's Choice, Carol, and FHL Reader's Choice. Her blog, *A Christian Writer's World*, which reaches more than 65,000 followers, received the Reader's Choice Blog of the Year Award from the Book Club Network.

Eva Marie Everson (evamarieeversonauthor.com) is a multiple-award-winning author and speaker. She has taught at a number of writers' conferences nationwide and serves as director of the Florida Christian Writers Conference and the North Georgia Christian Writers Conference (with Mark Hancock). She is the president of Word Weavers International Inc. and the managing editor of Firefly Southern Fiction, an imprint of Lighthouse Publishing of the Carolinas. Her 2017 novel, *The One True Love of Alice-Ann,* was in BookList's Top 10 List for Inspirational Fiction.

Suzanne Woods Fisher (suzannewoodsfisher.com) is an award-winning, best-selling author whose books have sold more than one million copies. She was recently featured in a Netflix/Buzzfeed documentary called *Follow Me,* about the popularity of Amish fiction. Her interest in the Plain People can be traced to her grandfather, who was raised Plain. Suzanne lives in the San Francisco Bay Area with her family.

Lori Freeland (lorifreeland.com) is an author, editor, and writing coach. She holds a BA from the University of Wisconsin and lives in the Dallas area. Former editor for *The Christian Pulse* and regular contributor to *Crosswalk.com,* she writes everything from nonfiction to short stories to novels from YA to adult. When she's not curled up on the couch next to her husband drinking too much coffee and worrying about her kids, she loves to mess with the lives of the imaginary people living in her head.

Renae Brumbaugh Green (RenaeBrumbaugh.com) is a best-selling author and award-winning journalist. Her best sellers are *Camp Club Girls and the Mystery at Discovery Lake* and *Christmas Stories for Bedtime.* She lives in Texas with her handsome country-boy husband, two nearly perfect children, and far too many animals.

Mona Hodgson (MonaHodgson.com) is the author of more than forty books, both historical novels for adults (including her popular

Sinclair Sisters of Cripple Creek series, The Quilted Heart novellas, and *Prairie Song*) and children's books, including *Bedtime in the Southwest, Real Girls of the Bible: A 31-Day Devotional*, six Zonderkidz "I Can Read" books, and six "I Wonder" books.

Angela Hunt (angelahuntbooks.com) is the author of more than one hundred works ranging from picture books to nonfiction to novels, with more than three million copies sold worldwide. Her books have won the Christy Award, several Angel Awards from Excellence in Media, and Gold and Silver Medallions from *Foreword* magazine's Book of the Year Award. In 2007, her novel *The Note* was featured as a Christmas movie on the Hallmark Channel. Romantic Times Book Club presented her with a Lifetime Achievement Award in 2006. When she's not home reading or writing, Angie often travels to teach writing workshops at schools and writers' conferences.

Julie-Allyson Ieron (joymediaservices.com) has published forty books. Her newest are *And There Were in That Same Country* and a second edition of her classic *The Overwhelmed Woman's Guide to Caring for Aging Parents*. Julie has the creative mind of a writer, the compassionate heart of a caregiver, the tenacity of a journalist, and the others-centeredness of an entrepreneur. All these come together in her multifaceted ministry of writing, editing, Bible teaching, worship leading, and caregiving.

Kathi Macias (kathimacias.com) is a multiple-award-winning writer who has authored more than fifty books and ghostwritten several others. A former newspaper columnist and string reporter, Kathi has taught creative and business writing in various venues and has been a guest on many radio and television programs.

Gail Gaymer Martin (gailgaymermartin.com) is an award-winning author of contemporary romance, sweet romance, and romantic suspense, with more than five million books sold. Her novels have received several national awards, including the Carol, RT Reviewers Choice, and Booksellers Best. Before writing fiction, Gail had hundreds of articles published in national magazines. She has taught English, literature, journalism, and public speaking at the high school and university levels. Raised in Michigan, Gail now lives in Sedona, Arizona, with her husband.

Susan Meissner (susanmeissner.com) is a multi-published author, speaker, and writing workshop leader with a background in community journalism. Her novels include *As Bright as Heaven* and *The Shape of Mercy*, named by Publishers Weekly as one of the 100 Best Novels of 2008.

Cecil Murphey (cecilmurphey.com) is the author or coauthor of 138 books, including *Gifted Hands: The Ben Carson Story* and *90 Minutes in Heaven*. His books for writers are *Unleash the Writer Within*, *Writer to Writer*, and *The Murphey Method of Ghostwriting*.

Deborah Raney (deborahraney.com) has written more than twenty books. Her first novel, *A Vow to Cherish*, inspired a World Wide Pictures film and launched her writing career after twenty happy years as a stay-at-home mom. Her books have won the RITA Award, ACFW Carol Award, the HOLT Medallion, National Readers' Choice Award, and Silver Angel. Two have been Christy Award finalists. She and her husband have four children and five grandchildren, who all live much too far away.

Gayle Roper (gayleroper.com) is the award-winning author of more than fifty books. She has been a Christy finalist three times. Her novel *Caught Redhanded* won the Carol Award, and *Autumn Dreams* won the Romance Writers of America's RITA Award for Best Inspirational Romance. Gayle has been awarded the HOLT Medallion three times. Romantic Times Book Report gave Gayle the Lifetime Achievement Award.

Cindy Woodsmall (cindywoodsmall.com) is a *New York Times* best-selling author who has written twenty-four works of fiction and one nonfiction book. Cindy has been featured on ABC-TV's *Nightline* and the front page of *The Wall Street Journal*, and she worked with National Geographic on a documentary concerning Amish life. In June 2013, *The Wall Street Journal* listed Cindy as one of the top three most popular authors of Amish fiction. She has won Fiction Book of the Year, Reviewer's Choice Awards, the Inspirational Reader's Choice Contest, and Crossings' Best Book of the Year. She's been a finalist for the prestigious Christy, RITA, and Carol Awards, Christian Book of the Year, and Christian Retailers Choice Awards.

Kathleen Y'Barbo (kathleenybarbo.com), a tenth-generation Texan and paralegal, is a multiple Carol Award and RITA nominee with more than one million copies of her ninety-plus books in print. Her awards include Book of the Year and Readers Choice Award nominations from *Romantic Times* magazine.

Made in the USA
Columbia, SC
25 September 2024